LANDSCAPES OF LEGEND

LANDSCAPES OF LEGEND

THE SECRET HEART OF BRITAIN

by

JOHN MATTHEWS

Photographs by Michael J. Stead

BLANDFORD

A BLANDFORD BOOK

First published in the UK 1997 by Blandford
A Cassell Imprint
Cassell plc, Wellington House,
125 Strand, London WC2R 0BB

Text copyright © 1997 John Matthews
Photographs copyright © 1997 Michael J. Stead
The rights of John Matthews and Michael J. Stead to be
identified as authors of this work has been asserted by them
in accordance with the provisions of the UK Copyright
Designs and Patents Act 1988.

Distributed in the United States by Sterling Publishing Co., Inc.,
387 Park Avenue South, New York, NY 10016-8810

A Cataloguing-in-Publication Data entry for this title is
available from the British Library

ISBN 0 7137 2650 4

Printed by Wing King Tong Co., Hong Kong

DEDICATION
To Jane Barnes and Liz O'Hamill,
Brave seekers after truth

Contents

Above: *Whitby Abbey, Yorkshire*
Opposite: *St Michael's Mount, Cornwall*

Frontispiece: *The, Merry Maidens Stone Circle, Cornwall*

INTRODUCTION
THE HIDDEN LAND

THE POET Gary Snyder tells a wonderful story of a journey across the outlands of Australia in an ancient truck, accompanied by a number of native people, one of whom was a story-teller. As they travelled, this man proceeded to tell a number of stories about the land through which they were passing. Every stone or hill or dried-up river-bed seemed to tell its own tale. As the truck bounced across the rough terrain the story-teller spoke faster and faster, and Snyder realized that he was listening to a verbal story-map of the land, which accelerated to match the speed of the truck.

To the Aboriginal people of Australia the land is a living thing, peopled with mysterious and magical beings; each place has its own story, its own fragment of the mythology of the land. The same is true, to a lesser extent, in places as widely separated as North America, Siberia and Japan. In Ireland there still exists a huge collection of topographical stories, collected under the title of the *Dindsenchas* (Land-lore), which relate the mythology of the land itself, its trees and hills and rivers and cliffs, each one with its own tale of magic, and of the gods and heroes of the Celtic peoples. A typical entry reads:

CLOENLOCH: Hither came to his death Cloen son of Ingor . . . who spent fame, whose home was Alba, rich in horses, was the first man, cheerful of countenance, that came with wealth to Erin. Cloen of the hard, curved swords, though he ransacked many a chilly coast, his fatal faintness came not on him till he reached Cloenloch. Hence men speak everywhere of 'cloenloch' – let not its name be hidden! A prince that was hacked by spear-play met his death finally here.
(The Metrical Dindsenchas, ed. and trans. by R.A.S. Todd)

Once, there may well have existed a similar collection of tales relating to Britain, but if so this has long been lost. What has remained, however, is contained in the folklore and tradition that remember the famous heroes, the battles and trysts believed to have happened at certain specific places. Though much of this has also begun to be lost, as the last people who recall the old tales die out without recording them, much still remains. Thus memorials exist which tell of the burial-place of the great Welsh poet Taliesin by the lonely shore of Lake Bala, or how a group of people dancing on the sabbath were turned to stone and became the Rollright Stones, near Oxford. Other sites are known to be faery hills, gateways, at certain times of the year, to the Otherworld. The Eildon Hills on the borders of Scotland and England, are long remembered as the place where Thomas the Rhymer met the Queen of Faery, and where centuries later the Reverend Robert Kirk vanished from mortal sight in the pursuit of the faery race which he had studied for most of his life.

To the ancient peoples of Britain, the earth was indeed sacred, given shape and form in the stories of otherworldly women who represented the soul of the land. So we read, again and again, of would-be kings who must establish a relationship with the land over which they were to rule, by marrying, in ancient ceremonies that come from the beginning of recorded history, the women who represented the sovereignty of the land. In Irish myth this is a particularly strong theme, as shown in the archetypal story of Niall of the Nine Hostages, who as a youth is tested for his fitness to rule Ireland when he encounters a horrifyingly hideous woman guarding a well. Only when he is able to kiss her does she reveal herself as Eriu, who embodies the sovereignty of Ireland, and turns into a beautiful woman whom Niall will symbolically marry – thus wedding himself to the land.

Stories such as these underlie much of the mythical lore of Britain, emphasizing the spiritual links with the land which were once the common bounty of all human beings. In recent times we have cut ourselves off from that heritage, and become dislocated in many ways from the life-giving energy that lies beneath our feet. Only in the last few years has this begun to change a little, as we become more aware of the needs of the land, and of our own responsibility towards the wonderful creation that surrounds us. Echoes of what we once knew and recognized are still held by the rocks and standing stones, in the ancient trackways, and above all in the stories which still cling to both the natural places and the man-made sites that lie waiting for the wanderer in every corner of Britain.

To walk the hills and roads of England, Scotland and Wales is to walk in an enchanted place, a place where one may, if one keeps one's eyes open, encounter strange and wondrous beings just around the next bend or behind the rustling trees of an old wood.

The writer Robert Holdstock speaks of this wonderfully when, in his own chronicle of the mysterious inner landscape of Britain, he writes of places in the land where the echoes of the past are loud and the cultural heritage of myth, legend and story come together to form 'mythagos', resonances of older times that may still be encountered in the ancient woodlands.

> . . . all life is surrounded by an energetic aura . . . In these ancient woodlands . . . the combined aura forms something far more powerful, a sort of creative field that can interact with our unconscious. And it's in the unconscious that we carry . . . the pre-mythago – that's myth imago, the image of the idealised form of a myth creature. The image takes on substance in a natural environment . . . Historians and legend-seekers argue about where Arthur of the

Britons, and Robin Hood really lived and fought, and don't realise that they lived in many sites.
(*Mythago Wood*, Gollancz, 1984)

From standing stones to medieval castles, from Iron-Age forts to sacred groves, the landscape of Britain is filled with the kind of magic that brings such mythic images to life. The poet A. E. Housman called it 'Merlin's Isle of Gramarye' – this being an ancient word for magic – and it is right that Britain should be associated with its greatest magician, one whose power and wisdom extended far beyond that of Arthurian times, and whose presence is still to be felt in many places in the countryside today.

The present book, a companion volume to *King Arthur's Britain*, published by Blandford in 1995, extends the pictorial odyssey undertaken there to include a far wider range of sites, from the standing stones of Brodgar in the Orkneys, to the wild and mysterious landscape of Dartmoor, taking in the rich and varied heritage of the legendary landscape of Britain, its castles, its woods and fields and ancient hedgerows, places where stories still cling and many mysteries remain as little understood today as they did hundreds of years ago. I have tried to make as representative a selection as possible of the hugely varied places that have attracted their own store of legend, while being both accessible to the traveller, and containing their own special magic. Though not a guide book, this volume is meant for all those who enjoy exploring the magical places of Britain, or who prefer to journey from the comfort of their own armchair, through the mediums of photography and text, and who feel drawn to the hidden places that exist alongside the modern roadways, housing estates and urban jungles of our time. To those who love the heritage of Britain, and who continue to believe in the mystery which is just below the surface of the land, this book is dedicated. May you continue to find the gold that gleams out from beneath every hedgerow, encircles every tree, and lies buried just below your feet, in the very stuff of the earth beneath you.

John Matthews

MAP SITES

1 THE MERRY MAIDENS; ST MICHAEL'S MOUNT; MEN-AN-TOL; TREREEN DINAS
2 MEN GURTA; PENHALE SANDS
3 TINTAGEL CASTLE
4 WELLS CATHEDRAL
5 ROBIN HOOD'S BUTTS; STANTON DREW STONE CIRCLE
6 THE CERNE ABBAS GIANT
7 KNOWLTON CIRCLES
8 THE GREAT HALL, WINCHESTER
9 ARUNDEL CASTLE
10 THE LONG MAN OF WILMINGTON
11 THE WHITE TOWER
12 SILBURY HILL; THE UFFINGTON WHITE HORSE; WEST KENNET LONGBARROW; WAYLAND'S SMITHY
13 AVEBURY
14 THE DEVIL'S DYKE
15 ROYSTON CAVE
16 WANDLEBURY DYKE
17 THE ROLLRIGHT STONES; THE WHISPERING KNIGHTS
18 KILPECK CHURCH
19 CAERLEON-UPON-USK
20 CRAIG Y DDINAS; KENFIG POOL
21 PISTYLL Y RHAEADR
22 BEDD TALIESIN
23 BALA LAKE; OWEIN GLYNDWR'S FOOTPRINT
24 SNOWDON AND THE LAKE OF GLASLYN; LLYN DDINAS; DINAS EMRYS
25 BRYN CELLI DHU
26 ST WINIFRID'S WELL, HOLYWELL
27 HAWKSTONE PARK, MONUMENT AND GROTTO
28 THOR'S CAVE; ROBIN HOOD'S STRIDE
29 ARBOR LOW HENGE; THE NINE STONES
30 SKIPTON CASTLE
31 SHERIFF HUTTON CASTLE
32 HELMSLEY CASTLE; WHEEL-DALE ROMAN ROAD
33 WHITBY ABBEY
34 RICHMOND CASTLE
35 PENDRAGON CASTLE
36 DURHAM CATHEDRAL
37 CASTLERIGG
38 CHESTERS ROMAN BATHHOUSE
39 PIERCEBRIDGE
40 THE EILDON HILLS
41 HADRIAN'S WALL
42 ROSSLYN CHAPEL
43 ABERFOYLE FAERY HILL; ROBERT KIRK'S GRAVE
44 CLAVA CAIRNS
45 CARN LIATH BROCH
46 THE RING OF BRODGAR; THE STONES OF STENNESS; GURNESS BROCH; MAES HOWE AND MAES HOWE RUNIC SLAB; ST MAGNUS CATHEDRAL
47 STIPERSTONES
48 WROXETER

CHAPTER ONE

DREAMS AND RITUALS

STONE CIRCLES AND STANDING STONES

*These downs look as if they were sown
with great stones, very thick, and in a dusky
evening they look like a flock of sheep;
one might fancy it to have been the scene where
giants fought with huge stones against
the Gods.*

John Aubrey, *c.* 1650

ALL ACROSS the landscape of Britain stalk great stone figures, as mysterious today as when they were erected, thousands of years ago, by a prehistoric people who sought to represent something of the vast forces which they knew, instinctively, existed within the earth. It was in order to tap into these forces, and to understand and interpret the mysteries of the heavenly realm, that they erected the mighty circles of standing stones, the avenues of megaliths, and the holed stones which still stand, and which still perform the same function, in the landscape of the late twentieth century.

Since the stones were erected, however, numerous theories have been put forward to account for their placing and uses. The most frequent contenders for their setting up remain the Druids, who are believed to have overseen the erection of many of the major circles from Stonehenge in Wiltshire to Brodgar in the Orkneys. Debate still rages hotly over this, and turns upon whether the Druids arrived in these islands with the Celts (with whom they are still much associated) or whether they formed an indigenous priesthood from far earlier times. Since the Druids left no written records (they eschewed the use of such a means to record their beliefs and relied instead on oral tradition and memory) we cannot really say with any certainty what the truth is. There are certainly a large number of references to Druidism within the Celtic traditions, but this still tells us only that at some time (quite early on) Druids were serving as a priesthood among the Celts. However, there is still a possibility that there was a native

school of priests within Britain before 500 BC, the approximate date at which the Celts arrived.

Whatever the truth, and the argument shows no sign of reaching a satisfactory conclusion, someone oversaw the building of these mighty monuments, and though it was clearly not the Druids of whom we can read in the writings of Greek and Roman authors, there is no reason to suppose that there was not an indigenous priesthood well established in the British Isles who taught their wisdom to the incoming people.

A more important question concerns the use to which the stone circles, mounds and standing stones were put. They have been called stone needles, marking the acupuncture points in the earth's energy system; solar and lunar observatories that enabled their builders to observe and chart the course of the sun and moon through the cycle of the ritual year; places of sacrifice and inurement; stone dream-chambers and vision-lodges; and much more besides.

One account of the building of Stonehenge attributes it to no lesser a person than Merlin, the great enchanter of the Arthurian court, who brought the stones across the sea from Ireland and erected them as a lasting memorial to a fallen king. The same story attributes their origin to Africa, and says that they had healing properties for anyone who bathed in water that had been poured over the stones – a belief that continued until the seventeenth century. Indeed, the notion of the ability of many of the stones to bring healing was widespread throughout the Middle Ages, when a great deal of the folklore associated

Pages 12 and 13:
Men-an-Tol Stones,
Cornwall.

with circles and megaliths was first recorded. How far back beyond this time the stories can be traced is uncertain, and there is little surviving evidence to suggest that any of it went much beyond the eleventh century.

The medieval world was a credulous one in many ways, with people ever willing (as indeed they are today if the viewing figures of TV shows like *The X Files* are to be believed) to accept the most extraordinary claims of these mysterious sites, the original use of which they no longer remembered. Thus the properties of stones like Men-an-Tol in Cornwall, which was believed to cure babies of various ailments, is echoed in Scotland at a holed stone near Balymeanoch in Argyll; while the toothache-curing properties of the chambered tomb at Carraif an Talaidh, also in Argyle, is topped by the Crick Stone in Avon which was said to heal children of rickets. Rituals connected with childbirth are found as far apart as the Orkneys (Stone of Odin), Kilquhane (County Cork) and Innismurray (County Sligo). While elsewhere the catalogue of stories attached to the stones grows longer – including stories of hidden treasure, stones that cannot ever be counted, stones that move of their own volition, tombs which become the burial-place of countless heroes from Arthur to Sir Francis Drake, and which were built by giants, or the Devil or the faery people – who are seen as dwelling in or around or

beneath so many of the ancient sites which we have visited in the compilation of this book.

The antiquity of such beliefs is recorded at least as far back as the fifth century, and continued throughout the ninth century, as the records of early Christian councils (Arles in 443, Tours in 567 and Nantes in 889) show. These all inveigh against pagan practices of worshipping at stones and trees, on hills and at springs and wells. Whether these practices were genuine reminders of much earlier ones, or a corrupt form of such traditions, is unlikely to be answered with certainty.

All that we can say, ultimately, is that these sites possess a curious power which still draws us to this day. To stand within any of the stone circles, or to touch one of the great standing stones, is to feel a special kind of energy which one may, perhaps, call the heartbeat of the earth. Attempts to measure this energy have been made, with varying degrees of success, in recent times. That the presence of *something* measurable has been found at so many of these ancient monuments is itself an indication that there is more to these ancient stones than can be expressed in a theoretic reconstruction of a distant time. The very antiquity of the stones makes it difficult – perhaps impossible – to say more. It is perhaps enough to go there and to feel for oneself the power of place, the subtle energy which can move one, however briefly, into an altered state.

The Ring of Brodgar

Orkney Islands, OS HY 294134

THIS REMARKABLE site has been described as a 'sun temple', just as the neighbouring Stones of Stenness (page 19) have been called a 'lunar temple'. They are undoubtedly part of a much larger ritual complex, laid out across the island with a tantalizing geometry. There were, at one time, 60 stones, placed at exact distances from each other, and forming an exact circle measuring 103.7 m (340 ft). According to the great scholar of megalithic sites, Professor Alexander Thom, this constitutes exactly 125 megalithic yards (a unit of measurement which he proposed as the standard megalithic unit of length, approximately equivalent to 82.9 cm (2¾ ft). The significance of the precise layout of these circles is uncertain now, though they are known to reflect a pattern created within the landscape by the rising and setting of the sun and moon. The name Brodgar or Brogar probably derives from one of the Norse conquerors of Orkney, who may have held the lands around that place. At one time local people used to make their marriage vows within the circle, and following this would clasp hands through a massive stone ring called the Odin Stone. This was destroyed by a local farmer in the 1800s, after which the old custom fell into disuse. Until a generation or so ago all the standing stones in Orkney were believed to be giants, given to dancing at night and finally caught out in the light of the sun, which turned them all to stone. To stand within this vast circle of stones, especially at the time of the midsummer solstice, when it virtually never grows dark, is to feel oneself once again closely in touch with our ancestors, giant or not, who created the stone rings, and with the natural world, the energies of which they did so much to focus.

The Stones of Stenness

Orkney Islands, OS HY 306126

L IKE THE Ring of Brodgar, mentioned on page 16, this powerful circle of standing stones, all that remains of a circle of 12, and curiously shaped as though they were pointing to some ancient cluster of stars, has a very definite alignment – in this case with the rising and setting of the moon. It is possible that they form a kind of lunar observatory, just as the adjacent circle is believed to have served the same function for solar observation. A knowledge of the cycles of sun and moon were of considerable importance to the megalithic peoples who built the circles, both for the purposes of the agricultural year, and as part of a ritual observation. As recently as the nineteenth century the stones were known as 'The Kirk (Church) of Stenness' and local people would go there for a period of four or five days in order to prepare for a wedding to come. As noted above, they then took themselves to Brodgar and finally to the nearby Stone of Odin, where vows were taken. It was also believed at the time that if sick people walked three times around the stones deosil (in the same direction as the sun) they would be cured.

The achievement represented by the erection of these massive stones, many of them weighing more than twenty tonnes, is almost unbelievable when measured by present-day standards. The excavation of the bank and ditch which surrounds the stones has been calculated to have involved some 50,000 man-hours in order to quarry the 1,250 tonnes of sandstone necessary to create it. Whatever the final purpose of these monuments is judged to be, the feat of engineering required to bring them into being is a testimony to the dedication of their original architects.

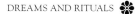

Castlerigg

Cumbria, OS NY 292236

ALSO KNOWN as the Keswick Carles, this group of stones is among the most dramatically situated in this part of the country. Crowning the spur of Chestnut Hill to the east of Keswick, the circle consists of 38 stones, arranged in a circle over 30 m (100 ft) in diameter to coincide with the rising and setting of the sun. According to Professor Alexander Thom, who studied the alignments of megalithic stone circles, this particular circle possesses a very complex mathematical layout, the precise purpose of which is no longer known. A psychometrist and psychic named Iris Campbell made the following observation in 1944:

> These stones were part of a Memorial Assembly Place where Kings came to mourn their dead. A central meeting place where Priests came from the surrounding Centres . . . performing their funeral rites by weaving different cosmic colours around the bier in order to spead the departure of the passing Soul.

Whether an oratory or an observatory, the stones have a powerful aura about them, which changes with the seasons and the weather. They are perhaps at their best in the snow, when the view on all sides is breathtaking. The name Keswick Carles suggests that they may at some time have had attached to them the familiar legends of dancing giants turned to stone; however, no such story seems to be remembered there today.

Avebury

Wiltshire, OS SU 103699

JUSTLY ONE of the most celebrated earth temples in Britain, Avebury rivals Stonehenge in the majesty of its construction and purpose. Much has been written about this site, from the earliest observations of the great antiquary William Stukeley, who sketched and described the monument in detail at the beginning of the eighteenth century, to the modern theories of Michael Dames, who has described Avebury and its surroundings as the remains of a still discernible mystery centre. There are some 98 sarsens (or Saracen's-stones), (the word may mean 'troublesome stones' from the Saxon *sar* and *stan*) surrounding two distinct smaller circles and a number of intermittently arranged groups of stones that may once have formed part of a greater pattern. For many years these have been recognized as being arranged in alternate 'male' and 'female' stones, which must at one time have been part of the ritual significance of the site.

A further avenue of stones curves away towards the West Kennet Long Barrow over 2.4 km (1½ miles) away. When the antiquarian John Aubrey (1626–97) visited the site in the mid seventeenth century it stretched even further, towards Overton Hill and a further small circle of stones known as 'The Sanctuary'. Another antiquarian, William Stukeley (1687–1765), recorded a second avenue, leading west towards Beckhampton. This has now largely vanished, but Stukeley's plan of the monument shows it in place, suggesting an intriguing serpentine shape which gave rise to speculations that Avebury in some way represented the sacred 'serpent energy' of the land.

Stukeley also attested to the fact that one group of stones, now called 'The Cove', were known as 'The Devil's Brand-irons', a typical example of the way that prehistoric and megalithic monuments were attributed to fiendish construction at the behest of early pagans. The massive Diamond Stone, lying west of the Swindon road, was believed to cross the road when the clock struck midnight – a belief still circulating until the beginning of the present century.

The sheer size of the monument leads one to suppose that it was a place of meeting and ritual celebration for a large part of the surrounding country. Given the comparatively small size of the population over the period of its construction, one can only wonder at the efforts required to excavate the massive banks and ditches (now only half their original depths) that stretch for more than 1.6 km (1 mile) around the circle. Add to this the movement and placing of the stones and one begins to get an idea of the dedication required over a duration of many years. The exact use of the site, beyond its obvious ritual significance, remains uncertain, though one writer, Mick Sharp, suggests that a statue of the local deity may have been kept hidden in the darkness of the sanctuary throughout the year, only to be brought forth and carried in ceremonial procession down the long avenue to the henge itself, where it would be set up and honoured by people from all over the area or even further away. One cannot be sure, but the awesome mystery of the place is so strong that few who visit it can fail to be moved.

The Merry Maidens

Cornwall, OS SW 433245

Men Gurta

Cornwall, OS SW 9668

THIS LITTLE group of 28 standing stones, set close to the road in a ploughed field, constitutes one of the most magical of the stone circles in this part of the land. Also known as the Dawns Men or Dancing Stones, they are a prime example of the many such sites that have acquired the legend of dancing people petrified in stone. Local belief, dating from at least as far back as 1730, tells that they were dancing to a piper, possibly of faery origin, on the sabbath, and that they were turned to stone as a punishment. Robert Hunt, the author of the eighteenth-century collection *Popular Romances of the West of England*, says that the music began slowly, but accelerated to the point where the dancers collapsed from exhaustion and became stones. Attempts to move the Merry Maidens have been recorded, but cattle employed to drag them away are said to have quickly fallen dead. The archaeologist and psychic researcher T.C. Lethbridge recorded his efforts to discover the date of the stones by using psychometry. He held a dousing pendulum in one hand and placed the other on one of the stones; at this point he felt a tingling sensation like a mild electric shock, while the pendulum swung out to an almost horizontal level and the stone felt as though it were shaking. This is typical of experiences recorded by a number of people.

STANDING ALONE on the side of St Breock Down, named after the Breton saint, is Men Gurta, or the Stone of Waiting, one of the most dramatic megaliths in the whole of the West Country. It stands on a small heap of quartz, and its surface is veined with more of the same substance, the existence of which at sacred sites is invariably associated with ritual. Its odd name seems curiously appropriate when one stands in front of it. It has the appearance of a very precisely appointed stone, which is indeed waiting – though for what one cannot say. As so often with stones of this kind, local tradition accounts for it as a petrified bolt of lightning or a stone dropped by a passing giant.

Left:
*The Merry Maidens
Stone Circle,
Cornwall.*

Opposite:
*Men Gurta Standing
Stone, Cornwall.*

Arbor Low Henge

Derbyshire, OS SK 160636

THIS MYSTERIOUS and dramatically situated circle, consisting of nearly 50 recumbent stones, has associations with ritual use that extend back to the days of the earliest settlers in this part of Britain. Traces of two ritual cremations were found near the centre of the present circle (which may have been built on the foundations of an earlier henge) as well as a 'food vessel', which may have contained offerings to the local gods. Several barrow mounds (burial sites), including one built into the side of the henge at a date several thousand years after its original construction, lie nearby, marking this site as one with a long and complex history. Modern 'ley hunters' (leys are energy conduits that flow across the land and connect sacred sites) have claimed that more than 50 ley-lines pass through this circle, possibly accounting for its powerful presence in the surrounding countryside. The nineteenth-century antiquary Thomas Bateman wrote in his *Vestiges of the Antiquities of Derbyshire* (1848):

> *Were it not for a few stone walls which intervene in the foreground, the solitude of the place and the boundless views are such as to almost carry the observer back through the multitude of centuries and make him believe that he sees the same view and the same state of things as existed in the days of the architects of this once holy place.*

This can stand as well for today as when it was written, except that the place is still very much 'holy'.

The Rollright Stones

Oxfordshire, OS SP 296308

AS THE folklorist Leslie Grinsell remarked some years ago, this stone circle has one of the richest traditional histories connected with any of the Stone-Age sites in Britain. The usual story of dancers turned into stone is told of the Rollrights, but with interesting variants. The seventeenth-century antiquarian William Camden wrote of the site in 1695 that it was:

> *A great monument of antiquity, a number of vastly great stones placed in a circular figure, which the country people call Rolle-rich stones, and have a fond tradition, that they were once men, thus turned into stones . . . The highest of them all, . . . they call the King; because they fancy he could have been king of England, if he could have seen Long Compton, a village within view at three or four steps further; five large stones, which upon one side of the circle touch one another, they pretend were the knights or horsemen; and the others common soldiers.*

In fact, this story is told of the adjacent group of stones known as the Whispering Knights (see page 31). Of the circle itself it is said that the stones never number the same twice – though anyone who can succeed in arriving at the same total three times will be rewarded with the granting of any wish he or she makes. It is also dangerous to take away any of the stones. Two men who attempted to do so just before the time of the Civil War were killed as the largest of the stones was dragged away from the circle. Needless to say it was soon replaced! Another man could find no rest after having taken one of the stones to make a footbridge over a nearby stream. The stones today look battered, partly due to weathering and partly due to vandalism.

The Whispering Knights

Oxfordshire / Warwickshire, OS SP 296309

THE STORY TOLD on page 28 refers not to the Rollrights themselves, but to the adjacent Whispering Knights, so called because they lean inwards, giving the impression of having their heads together. The King Stone (which is actually just over the border in Warwickshire) is said to go down to the nearby spring in Little Rollright Spinney when the clock strikes twelve. The story of the petrified stones was later elaborated to include the nameless king's encounter with a witch or seeress who said to him:

Seven long strides shalt thou take, and
If Long Compton thou canst see,
King of England shalt thou be.

However, before he could take more than six strides, a mound rose up before the king, preventing him from seeing the village. Whereat the seeress said:

As Long Compton thou canst not see,
King of England thou shalt not be.
Rise up, stick, and stand still, stone,

For King of England thou shalt be none,
Thou and thy men hoar stone shall be,
And I myself an eldern tree.

According to some accounts the witch in question was the redoubtable 'Mother Shipton' who lived at nearby Milton-under-Wychwood from the end of the fifteenth century to the beginning of the seventeenth century. In the nineteenth century people would circle the King Stone on Midsummer's Eve, when the elder (eldern) tree flowered. The tree was then cut, and appeared to bleed, at which point the King Stone moved its head. Another story tells that one day the king and his men will awaken and march forth to conquer England.

Stanton Drew Stone Circle

North-east Somerset (formerly Avon), OS ST601633

THIS SITE is really a complex of ritual monuments, including not only a circle of massive stones but also an avenue and cove of smaller stones reminiscent of Avebury Henge (see pages 22–3). In common with nearly every stone circle of its kind there is a myth of petrifaction attached to the site.

The Nine Stones

Derbyshire OS SK 227625

A wedding party met there once, and a fiddler began his merry tunes. As the time neared midnight and the sabbath was about to dawn, a mysterious dark stranger appeared and took over the music. As the hours passed and the dancing continued the people realized that this was no ordinary fiddler, but the Devil himself. As dawn came the revellers were turned to stone, and the Devil's last words to them was a promise that one day in the future he would return and play again. Until that moment they wait, frozen in stone. A great stone, once known as the Fiddler is now called Hautville's Quoit, after the fourteenth-century landowner Sir John Hautville, who is believed to have tossed it onto its present location from nearby Norton Hill. As with the Rollright Stones (see pages 28–9) it is said that no one could count the stones in the circle and arrive at the same number. As the seventeenth-century antiquarian John Wood remarked in his *Description of Bath*:

> No one, say the country people about Stantondrue, was ever able to reckon the number of these metamorphosed stones, or to take a draught of them, though several have attempted to do both, and proceeded till they were either struck dead upon the spot, or with such an illness as soon carried them off.

If left to themselves and uncounted, the stones have a powerful, rather sleepy feel to them, as though the dancers had grown tired of their endless gyration, and had drifted off to sleep . . .

ALSO KNOWN as the Grey Ladies, these stones are actually nine in number, unlike many other such circles or collections of standing stones, which seem to have been given the name arbitrarily due to the association of nine with good luck. (Nine, like seven, is traditionally a lucky number.) Again like many of the circles included here, the Nine Stones have attracted the old story of people dancing on the sabbath and being turned to stone as a punishment. One suggestion which has been put forward to explain this is that certain stones are said to dance at midday while others do so at midnight. At one time the ninth canonical hour of the day in ecclesiastical reckoning was at three in the afternoon, when the service of 'nones' was celebrated. This was later moved to midday, but the name remained, from which we have our current word 'noon'. The fact that 'none' was still remembered as the ninth hour then became attached to the nine stones, and the legend followed along in due course.

The stones themselves are very weathered now, but they still retain a powerful atmosphere, especially as dusk is falling, and the sun vanishes behind the edge of Harthill Moor. Like many of the stone circles pictured here, the Nine Stones demonstrates the importance of alignments which mirrored the patterns of sun, moon and stars.

Men-an-Tol

Cornwall, OS SW 427349

THIS REMARKABLE holed stone lies in the depths of a most enchanted part of the land, not far from Madron's Well, a place long associated with healing and possibly dedicated to Modron, an ancient mother goddess of the Celts. Local tradition speaks of the healing and magical properties of the stone through which ailing children were passed a number of times (usually nine), girls passed from man to woman, boys from woman to man. The celebrated historian and antiquary William Borlaise visited Men-an-Tol in 1749, and was told by a local farmer that many people crept through the stone when seeking a cure for back pains or rickets. It was also said that if two brass pins were laid on top of the stone, they acquired a curious mobility which enabled them to answer questions put to the stone according to how they spun. Couples about to marry would often visit the stone, and the woman, on climbing through it, was certain to bear healthy children. The two stones set on either side of the central stone suggest that it was originally used as a means of estimating the rising and setting of either solar or lunar events.

CHAPTER TWO

GUARDING THE LAND

HILL FIGURES, FORTS AND ROMAN WAYS

*Before the gods that made the gods
Had seen their sunrise pass
The White Horse of the White Horse Vale
Was cut out of the grass.*

G.K. Chesterton, 'The Ballad of the White Horse'

*A man in chalk, formed under first starglow,
Recording history from ancestral start;
He listens close, as one who waits should know.*

Caitlin Matthews, 'Long Man Listening'

THE IDEA of magically guarding Britain goes back a very long way. One of the old names for Britain is Merlin's Enclosure, described in later tales as a wall made of brass that encircled the entire island, protecting it from invasion. This is restated in the story of Bran the Blessed (see Chapter 4) who, as his death neared, ordered his followers to cut off his head and bury it beneath a certain hill with the face towards France. As long as it remained there, no one would succeed in breaching the defences of the island. The truth of this was never really put to the test, since the warrior Arthur later ordered the head exhumed on the grounds that he, and he alone, could guard Britain. Soon after, despite all Arthur's efforts, the Saxons did invade, and once Arthur had departed (himself interred within the land as its tutelary guardian) they made this land at least partly their own.

Long before this time, other guardian figures bestrode the land. Designs cut into the chalk hillsides of southern Britain seem to have marked early attempts to lay claim to the earth and to warn of those who might seek to take it for their own. The most famous of these is the Uffington White Horse (see pages 40-1), in length a massive 114-m (374-ft) image carved out of the Berkshire Downs. The true reason for its presence there remains a mystery, though a number of theories – some persuasive, some less so – have been put forward. By some it is held to have been the sign of the local Dobruni tribe, whose coins, found in the area, bear the symbol of a horse similar in many ways to the Uffington image. If this is the case then the White Horse may have marked either a boundary or a place of central importance to the tribe. The Uffington hill-fort which lies just above the figure may have been constructed by the same people. However, recent archaeological investigation suggests that the horse is in fact older than the fort – though it may date from the same time as the barrow mounds also found nearby. That the site was recognized as somehow sacred is indicated by the efforts made to keep it cleared of the gradual encroachment of grass and soil across the hillside. Chesterton's 'Ballad of the White Horse' describes this vividly:

> The turf crawled and the fungus crept,
> And the little sorrel, while all men
>   slept,
> Unwrought the work of man.
> With velvet finger, velvet foot,
> The fierce soft mosses then
> Crept on the large white commonweal
> All folk had striven to strip and peel,
> And the grass like a great green witch's
>   wheel,
> Unwound the toils of men.

These invasions of the White Horse were, until quite recent times, kept at bay by an annual 'scouring' of the image, which took place (usually in September) as part of a general celebration that included a fair and sports. The novelist Thomas Hughes, famous for *Tom Brown's Schooldays*, wrote a novel, *The Scouring of the White Horse* (1857), which tells of this.

Other famous hill figures include the Long Man of Wilmington, who stands with arms spread wide on the steep escarpment of Windover Hill, (see page 42) and the mighty Cerne

Previous pages:
*The Devil's Dyke,
Hertfordshire.*

Abbas Giant, who stands with upraised club on a hillside in Dorset (see page 43). Despite numerous attempts to explain their purpose, they are really as mysterious today as they ever were. To me it seems most likely that, like the head of Bran, these huge figures in the landscape were an expression of the energy of the land itself, and stood as guardians for all who dwelled within Merlin's Enclosure.

Long after their true purpose had been forgotten, other people trod the sacred outline of the land and made their own kind of defences to impress their claim to rulership on the indigenous population. The Roman conquest of Britain was never really total – many areas remained purely British, and when the last of the legions departed in AD 410 the land very quickly returned to something not unlike it had been before.

Nevertheless, Rome left her mark on the land, and we can still see the remains of this presence in the forts, roads and most of all the great wall built at the behest of the Emperor Hadrian (see pages 52–3) which was intended both to keep in the Britons and keep out the Picts.

Natural barriers such as the haunted peaks of Snowdon (see pages 44–5) or the various Devil's Dykes (see page 46), complete this aspect of the legendary landscape. But whether one thinks of the Uffington horse, the giants of Cerne Abbas and Wilmington, the Roman walls or the frozen rocks of Snowdonia, there is a common thread that connects them all. The land is, as it was to our ancestors, still a sacred place, and sacred places need signs and guardians to remind us of the fact. All of the images presented here are, in their own way, such reminders. To look at them is to see beyond them into the mystery of the land itself, with all its memorials to other days, which are still only a heartbeat away from us, if we look and listen carefully enough.

The Uffington White Horse

Wiltshire, OS SU 302866

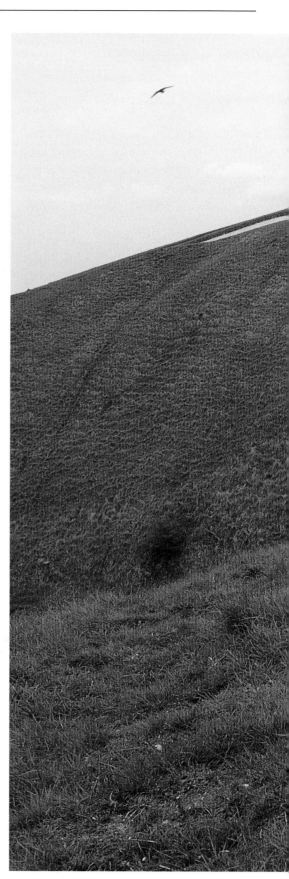

O F ALL the mighty chalk hill figures that decorate the landscape of southern Britain this is, to me, the finest. Graceful, powerful and proud, the White Horse, 114 m (374 ft) long and cut from the turf on the chalk hillside, somehow encapsulates the qualities of the land itself and the many generations of ancient folk who have lived upon it. Less than a mile away runs the Ridgeway, an ancient prehistoric trackway that connects with a number of sites of ritual importance, including Wayland's Smithy (see page 123), West Kennet Long Barrow (see page 22) and Avebury (see page 22–3), and which remains an important carrier for the hidden energy of the land. The stylized shape of the horse has lead to a good deal of speculation as to its actual identity. There are those who have suggested it may be in fact a dragon, an idea backed up by the presence of Dragon Hill, which lies just below it. A bald path on top of this hill, where neither grass nor weeds will grow, is said to be the site of St George's battle with the dragon, for which reason the hilltop is forever barren. Others have pointed out that the likeness of the 'horse' appears on numerous coins of the Dobruni and Atrebates tribes, found in the area. The presence of an Iron-Age hill-fort (Uffington Castle) adjacent to the Horse has also been brought into the argument as being the probable home of those who carved the hill figure from the chalk. If this theory is correct, then it is possible that the White Horse represents the goddess Epona, sacred to the Celts and worshipped in the form of a horse or a woman seated on a horse. However, recent archaeological investigations of the site revealed that the horse may date from much earlier than Celtic times – successive layers of chalk infill were discovered, indicating that a succession of horses pranced across the hillside, possibly as early as 2000 BC. This would make the Uffington horse the oldest such chalk hill figure still extant in Britain. Certainly, to walk there is to feel an extraordinary power, while to sit within the eye of the horse has long been considered a likely source of vision. To look out from this vantage point across the curve of the 'Manger' and south across the Vale of the White Horse is to feel especially connected to the spiritual heritage of ancient Britain.

The Long Man of Wilmington

Sussex, OS TQ 543034

THIS REMAINS one of the most mysterious of the chalk hill figures that are found throughout southern Britain. Said by some to be a doorkeeper, opening the way between the worlds, and by others to be a solar cult figure who once held up sun discs on the top of his two staves, the Long Man has refused to be categorized or identified in any definite way. Much has been made of the dimensions of the figure. He stands 70.4 m (231 ft) tall and his two staves measure 71.6 m (235 ft) each. The precision of these measurements has led some commentators to see the Long Man as an image of the archetypal surveyor, perhaps one of those who first charted the system of ley-lines (conduits of energy that criss-cross the land). The presence of a large number of neolithic and Stone-Age sites in the immediate area suggest that the Long Man may have possessed considerable ritual importance for the people living in the area. The hillside on which the figure stands is pocked with marks which are all that remains of ancient flint mines. A local legend has transformed this into the signs of a battle between giants – those of Wilmington and nearby Firle. The two were said to have fought by throwing boulders at each other, which made the dents in the earth. The Wilmington giant lost and lies buried beneath the hillside. This makes the chalk figure a memorial of the dead giant, and it may well be that behind this lies a story of a titanic battle between two heroes, one of whom was subsequently buried there. Rodney Castleden, the only modern authority to study the figure in depth, suggests that it commemorates an ancient ritual of the summer solstice, with the giant as a kind of solar hero, battling against the darkness of the winter god. Whatever theory one chooses, there is no denying the power of this ancient figure, who guards the way to the mysteries of the land and opens doors within the imagination of all who confront him.

The Cerne Abbas Giant

Dorset, OS ST 667016

THE CERNE GIANT has probably been identified with more disparate characters than any of the great guardian hill figures that have survived. To some he is Hercules, to others the ancient British giant Gog, while still others regard him as simply a nameless fertility symbol. But the question of who carved him and why has still to be answered satisfactorily. His ithyphallic stance and upraised club suggest a warrior or hero, possibly of the Celtic or proto-Celtic peoples of Britain, and there is a strong tradition that women who sleep within the outline of the figure – especially within the phallus – will be blessed with fertility.

A small earthwork enclosure on Trendle Hill, above the giant's head, was until the beginning of the century the site of May Day revels. For this a huge maypole was set up and celebrations, including a fair and sports, were held around the first of the month. These celebrations, which can be traced back to Celtic or even earlier times, suggest both a connection with fertility (the underlying theme of the revels) and with the turning of the ancient agricultural year. William Stukeley, the great seventeenth-century antiquarian, was under no doubt that the figure was Hercules, the leader, as he would have it, of Phoenician tin miners who settled in Britain before the coming of the Romans!

Other possibilities would include the eponymous Celtic deity Cernunnos, the lord of the animals, whose name might be supposed to be reflected by the name of Cerne Abbas. However, since this figure is almost invariably represented as horned, and since no trace of horns has

been found at the site of the giant, this must be doubtful. Some kind of native deity, possibly related to fertility, therefore still seems the best bet, while the fact that the giant's 9-m (30-ft) phallus is directly aligned with the rising sun on May Day, seems to strengthen the ritual connection with the magical celebrations taking place on the hill above his head. Ultimately, like his fellow giant at Long Wilmington in Sussex (see page 42), he may be perceived as a guardian of the land, his presence stating beyond question that beyond him lies an otherworldly place of wonder and magic.

Snowdon and the Lake of Glaslyn

Wales, OS SH 6154

THE SNOWDON range is surely the most fearsome and powerful barrier to be encountered in the whole western part of Britain. It successfully kept out various succeeding invaders: Roman, Saxon and Norman, and remained for the Celts an enclave against loss of cultural identity – which is still true to this day. The fifteenth-century poet Rhys Goch Eryri, who lived in the shadows of Snowdon, wrote 'On the ridge cold and vast, there the giant Ricca lies'. This Ricca is better known as Rhita Gawr, who appears in the Arthurian legends as an opponent of Arthur who bore a cloak trimmed with the beards of kings he had overcome. He sent a message to Arthur, demanding that his beard should be added to the decoration. Arthur refused and Rhita challenged him to a battle on the summit of Snowdon. Arthur accepted, defeated and killed Rhita, and won the marvellous cloak for himself. In the nineteenth century there was still a cairn to be seen near the summit of the mountain, which was known locally as *Carnedd y Cawr* (the Giant's Cairn). It was later demolished and made into a kind of tower, which stood on the site for a number of years until it, too, gave way to a hotel. This story has been cited as originating with the older name for Snowdon, *yr Wyddfa Fawr*, (the Great Tomb), which is still remembered in the name of a steep cliff face called *Clogwyn Carnedd yr Wyddfa* (the Precipice of the Carn on yr Wyddfa). Arthur himself is remembered as sleeping in a cave beneath the mountain, not far from the giant's grave at a place called the Pass of the Arrows. This is only one of numerous sites associated with Arthur, and designated as the site of his grave, but it may explain the idea of an important character buried somewhere within the body of the mountain. Arthur is also described as a giant in more than one folk story, though he probably replaced an older figure.

Llyn (Lake) Glaslyn, a still, dark pool of water on the western flank of the mountain, is rumoured to be bottomless and has a story both of the giant's treasure being thrown into it and of a monster lurking in its depths. Whether either of these tales has any foundation, or is simply a later addition to the story of the battle fought on the slopes of yr Wyddfa, remains uncertain, though since the lake is almost certainly a product of mining work in the area, the authenticity of the stories remains doubtful.

The Devil's Dyke

Hertfordshire, OS TL 184135

THIS STRIKING site, a massive 12 m (40 ft) deep and 27.4 m (90 ft) wide, is probably all that remains of an Iron-Age fortified camp, and may once have been the headquarters of the Celtic leader Cassivellaunus, defeated by Julius Caesar in 54 BC. It is one of many such places, either natural formations or the misunderstood remains of an older site, which have received the name and reputation of devilish workmanship.

Above:
Devil's Dyke,
Hertfordshire.

Right:
Wandlebury Dyke,
Cambridgeshire.

Wandlebury Dyke

Cambridgeshire, OS TL 493534

THIS SITE, together with the adjacent Wandlebury Camp and the nearby Gogmagog Hills, are linked to an intriguing story and a possible lost hill figure of the same type as the Cerne Abbas Giant (page 43) and the Long Man of Wilmington (page 42). The dyke itself is actually part of the original ramparts of the Iron-Age camp. The medieval writer Gervase of Tilbury (*c.* 1212) recorded the following:

There is a very ancient tradition, attested by popular report, that if a warrior enters this level space at dead of night, when the moon is shining, and cries 'Knight to Knight come forth!', immediately he will be confronted by a warrior, armed to fight, who, charging horse to horse, either dismounts his adversary or is dismounted. But I should add that the warrior must enter the enclosure alone, although his companions may look on from outside.

There is some evidence to suggest that the actual site of this encounter took place in the dyke rather than on the hill-fort itself, though the truth will probably never be known. During the 1950s the archaeologist T. C. Lethbridge claimed to have discovered, on the chalk escarpments of the Gogmagog Hills, the remains of a vast hillside panorama, consisting of the giant Gog and the Celtic horse goddess Epona. He further suggested that fertility rites may have been carried out here at one time, as at Cerne Abbas and Uffington. Although this theory was received with little interest by the academic community, there were undoubted signs of some kind of hill figure at the site, and although this is now grown over, the enigma remains. References to such a figure are to be found in a number of seventeenth- and eighteenth-century texts, and at last one of these suggested that the phantom knight who is to be encountered at Wandlebury, may be the same as the giant once carved in the chalk of the hillside.

Caerleon-Upon-Usk

Wales, OS ST 340906

THIS SITE has a long and venerable history spanning several centuries. Its original name seems to have been Caer Usk (City of the Usk), but it was widely known as Caer-Leon (City of the Legions) during the Roman occupation of the area. The Romans themselves called it Isca Silurum, after the local tribe of the Silures. It was the headquarters of the 2nd Augustan Legion from around AD 75 and served as the administrative centre for South Wales during this time. The remains of the Roman fortress, which include bathhouses and a magnificent amphitheatre, are one of the best-preserved sites of this kind anywhere in the country, while its legendary associations are fascinating. Geoffrey of Monmouth, the erstwhile chronicler of Arthurian Britain, called Caerleon 'the Mother of Cities' in South Wales, and made it Arthur's greatest city, more important even than the better-known Camelot. At one time a green mound covered the site of the amphitheatre, and this was known locally as King Arthur's 'Round Table' (one of many such places to bear this name across the country). In *History of the Kings of Britain* (*c.* 1136) Geoffrey describes it in glowing terms as:

> *Situated in a passing pleasant position . . . and abounding in wealth above all other cities, it was the place most meet for so high a solemnity* [the crowning of Arthur]. *For on one side there flowed the noble river* [Usk] *whereby the Kings and Princes that should come from overseas might be born thither in their ships, and on the other side, girdled about with meadows and woods, passing fair was the magnificence of the kingly palaces thereof with the gilded verges of the roofs that imitated Rome.*

While this deals with the myth-laden image of the medieval Arthur, Geoffrey is actually recalling much earlier Celtic traditions, which support the association of Arthur with Caerleon. In the romance traditions that followed in the later Middle Ages, the city became known as Segontium, and was associated with the quest for the Grail.

Piercebridge

Northumberland, OS NZ 2115

THE GREAT system of Roman roads spanned Britain in a series of vital lifelines. These connected with the great forts from which the Roman government did their best to control the wild and wayward Celts. Here at Piercebridge, situated half-way along the surviving length of Dere Street, one of the last surviving Roman bridges spanned the River Tees, until its course changed sometime in the early years of the twentieth century. Here, according to local tradition, on certain nights one may still hear the echoing tread of the legions, marching through the almost vanished ruins of the Roman fort that lie near to the road.

Hadrian's Wall

Cumbria and Northumberland

OS NY 2661, 3757, 4561, 7167, 8069 and NZ 0568

HADRIAN'S WALL, begun at the behest of the Emperor Hadrian (reigned AD 117–38) around AD 120 and finally abandoned in AD 383, is surely the greatest testimony to the presence of Roman rule in Britain. It was made to keep out Pictish tribesmen, and to mark the most extreme northern frontier of the Roman Empire. It extended originally from Wallsend, near Newcastle-upon-Tyne, to Bowness-on-Solway on the Solway Firth. Originally 116.8 km (73 miles) long, 3 m (10 ft) wide, 4.5 m (15 ft) high and topped with 1.8 m (6 ft) of timber and stone battlements, the wall must have been a formidable barrier then as indeed it still is today. Much of it still survives, crowning hillsides in Cumbria and Northumberland, the remains still as much as 4.2 m (14 ft) high. Ruined turrets, milecastles and forts still mark its powerful presence, and many are said to be haunted, either by the Roman legionaries who fought and died there, or by other figures deriving from local lore and legend. Though it took 10,000 men eight years to build, the Scottish wizard Michael (or Mitchell) Scott was at one time believed to have built the wall in a single night with the help of the Devil – presumably at a time when knowledge of Roman artefacts was almost non-existent! Where the wall runs along the spine of Sewingsheild's Craggs towards Housesteads, local legend points to a massive 20-tonne boulder, lying at the foot of the Craggs, as being thrown there by a giant King Arthur after a quarrel with a giant Queen Guinevere. But it is the wall itself that one remembers, powerful and even menacing at times, an unforgettable reminder of the presence of the Roman legions.

Wheeldale
Roman Road

Yorkshire, OS SE 7997

THIS STRETCH of Roman road runs across the bleak moorland at Wheeldale in North Yorkshire. Intended to link the nearby Roman camps to the garrison town of Malton, local tradition has given it another name and history. Known widely as Wade's Causeway, the road was supposedly built by two giants, Wade and his wife Bell, who are together responsible for some remarkable feats of building work. They are attributed with the construction of both Pickering and Mulgrave castles, while this stretch of roadway was said to have been made in single day, with Wade laying the stones as his wife carried them in her apron. Once or twice she dropped some, thus explaining the occasional heaps of rocks found by the roadside. Wade may in fact be the father of Wayland, the mysterious smith of the gods whose smithy can still be see in Oxfordshire near the Ridgeway (see page 123).

The ancient Roman road at Wheeldale, Yorkshire.

Chesters Roman Bathhouse

Northumberland, OS NY 9171

ALITTLE TO the north of Hadrian's Wall, on the banks of the North Tyne river, stands this remarkably preserved Roman military bathhouse, once heated by a complex system of hot-air channels, where the legionaries would have performed their ablutions before returning to duty in the adjacent fort of Cilurnum. This fort, garrisoned by the 2nd Asturian Horse, a cavalry regiment, was one of the largest in the this part of the country, and must have emphasized the presence of the legions and the Roman way of life particularly strongly to the native tribes of the area. As with so many of the ruined forts along Hadrian's Wall, Chesters has its share of ghosts, with Roman soldiers seen patrolling their old guard posts as though the Roman legions had never left.

Above:
The wall of the bathhouse at Chesters, Northumberland.

Wroxeter

Shropshire, OS SJ 5608

THESE FEW tumbled walls and pillars are all that remains of the once thriving Roman city of Viroconium Cornoviorum (now known as Wroxeter) which, during the first few years of Roman rule in Britain, served as a military base from which the attempted conquest of South Wales was to take place. Perhaps because of the failure of the legions to penetrate the hills and valleys where the Cornovii had taken refuge, the centre of administration was moved, around AD 78, to Chester, after which Viroconium became a civilian town. At one time it covered an area of 72 ha (180 acres), and included law courts, a large bathhouse, a central market-place and basilica. There is some evidence to suggest that before the Romans developed the site, it may have been an important settlement of the Cornovii, and that after the departure of the legions in AD 410 it became the capital of the newly formed province of Powys.

A recent theory suggests that it may have been one of the most important bases for the Arthurian defence of Britain, and the authors of this idea, Graham Phillips and Martin Keatman, have described Viroconium as 'the real Camelot'. In fact, archaeological excavations in the 1960s did show that the city was reconstructed during the fifth century, more than 100 years after the departure of the Roman legions. This suggests that a Dark-Age leader made the city his capital – in which case the most likely contender would be Vortigern rather than Arthur. Whatever the truth, the ruins are still a reminder that the Romano-British settlements that remained after AD 410 did not abandon the culture they had inherited from their Roman masters, but developed it in their own unique way.

Gurness Broch

Orkney Islands, OS HY 383268

To THE Iron-Age people of Britain the Orkney Islands were a sacred place, synonymous with the Isles of the Dead. All over the islands are tombs, dating from Stone Age to megalithic and, not surprisingly, there had to be places of guardianship established. The coastline of the islands is protected by a series of curious stone towers, called brochs, like this one at Gurness on the north shore of the main Orkney island. Its walls are a massive 2.4 m (8 ft) thick; it is some 4.5 m (15 ft) in diameter and contains a well of fresh water. The brochs are unlike any other remains from this period and seem to have evolved independently of any similar constructions. More than 500 were built across the north of Britain and on the islands around Scotland. They were mostly double-skinned, rose to as much as 7.6 m (25 ft) in height, and were built of dry-stone walling to a most sophisticated degree of architecture.

Gurness Broch was discovered by the Orkney poet Robert Rendall, who was sketching one day in the summer of 1929 when one of the legs of his chair sank into the earth. Curious, he removed some stones from near where he had been sitting and found a stair descending beneath ground level. Excavations showed the broch had been in use for many hundreds of years, possibly as late as the Viking period, and a number of buildings were uncovered, together with a triple row of banks and ditches.

Carn Liath Broch

Scotland, OS NC 870013

ARN LIATH, the Grey Carn, is a type of broch (see opposite) which at one time rose to as high as 4.5 m (15 ft) and had walls over 2.4 m (8 ft) thick. The remains can still be seen today, overlooking the Sutherland coast. Building of the brochs began as early as 1000 BC, and developed from earlier, more primitive structures over a number of years. Though primarily defensive in purpose, there is a possibility that they may have been used as 'dream' towers, where seers might lie and watch the clouds or stars (the brochs were generally open to the sky or only partly thatched) from within the safety of the massive walls.

CHAPTER THREE

THE MEMORY OF THE LAND

TIME PAST AND TIME FUTURE

Thou genius of this place (this most renowned isle)
Which livedst long before the All-earth-
drowning Flood,
Whilst yet the world did swarm with her
Gigantic brood;
Go thou before me still thy circling shores about,
And in this wandering maze help to conduct me out.

Michael Drayton, *Poly-Olbion*

WHEREVER WE go in Britain we see visible reminders of the past. Whether they are ancient field boundaries, dating from the time of neolithic farmers, or the walls and ditches of Iron-Age forts, each place has its own story to tell. The same is true of the landscape itself, where so many hills, caves and pools of water have their own stories. It is here that the great heroes of the land are remembered, people such as Robin Hood, King Arthur, Hereward the Wake, and Owein Glendwyr, whose names cling to the very rocks and earth where they once walked, as though their spirits, having sunk back into the land that gave them birth, have left behind a more lasting memorial, expressed in the living landscape.

Although it tends to be folk memory that has preserved the legends of place, literature has also played its part. Malory's great epic 'novel' of Arthur (*Le Morte d'Arthur*) records the fact that Winchester was Camelot (see Chapter 4), while the Eildon Hills and the faery hill at Aberfoyle (see page 72) are remembered in the ballad of Thomas the Rhymer and the writings of Sir Walter Scott, or in the works of the great folk-lore collectors of the eighteenth and nineteenth centuries. Thus one can hardly walk the hills near the river Tweed, where Thomas met the Queen of Faery, without recalling the words of his ballad:

Previous pages:
Robin Hood's Butts,
Somerset.

> *True Thomas lay on Huntley Bank,*
> *A wonder spied he with his eye;*
> *And there he spied a lady bright*
> *Come riding down by the Eildon tree*

> *Her shirt was of the grass-green silk*
> *Her mantle of the velvet fine;*
> *At every tuft of her horse's mane*
> *Hung fifty silver bells and nine.'*

Similarly, to visit the grave of the Reverend Robert Kirk, in the churchyard of Kirkton, is to recall the story of his disappearance, some say into the faery hill itself, where perhaps he still dwells, hoping that someone will remember him and call him back to the world of men.

Not only the good people are remembered in the land. A number of natural formations, such as the Stiperstones (pages 78–9), which lie along the back of a rocky rise in the Shropshire hills, are said to be the work of the Devil – who is indeed remembered almost as often as certain heroes in places as far apart as Buckinghamshire (the Devil's Barrow), Cornwall (the Devil's Quoit), and Northumberland (the Devil's Lapful). Here we may suspect the presence of earlier stories of local deities, whose names and identities have been subsumed by later Christian story-tellers. The Devil is also seen to be responsible for the turning into stone of people unwise enough to dance on the sabbath, as the many stories which tell of Old Nick playing the fiddle for such carousals will bear witness.

Villages too, like those which lie beneath Penhale Sands (see page 87) or Bala Lake (see page 127) can be drowned in a moment if their inhabitants behave foolishly or wickedly, and more than one still pool of water hides crumbling walls, or church towers from which the dim echo of bells may still be heard on certain quiet nights.

The land remembers all of these things, as the great Celtic visionary 'AE' wrote so eloquently in his book *The Candle of Vision* (Quest Books, 1965):

> *. . . we are led to believe that memory is an attribute of all living creatures and of Earth also, the greatest living creature we know, and that she carries with her, and it is accessible to us, all her long history, cities far gone behind time, empires which are dust, or are buried with sunken continents beneath the waters. The beauty for which men perished is still shining; Helen is there in her Troy, and Deirdre wears the beauty which blasted the Red Branch. No ancient lore has perished. Earth retains for herself and her children what her children might in passion have destroyed, and it is still in the realm of the Ever Living to be seen by the mystic adventurer.*

It is we, indeed, who are the mystic adventurers, as we walk the land in the quest of its mysteries and its wisdom.

Silbury Hill

Wiltshire, OS SU 100685

SILBURY IS one of the largest man-made mounds anywhere in the world. It rivals the pyramids of Giza and the earth mounds of North America in size and complexity of construction – and yet no one knows with any real certainty why it was put there. Theories abound, as do legends and folklore – the hill has been the subject of question and debate for several hundred years. Dating from around 2700 BC, it is fashioned from hundreds of tonnes of earth, faced with chalk and covered by turf. It covers an area of almost 2 ha (5¼ acres) at base; is 40 m (130 ft) high and probably took two centuries to complete (according to the latest calculations the equivalent of 700 men working for ten years).

Since the time of Stukeley in the eighteenth century there has been a local legend which tells that a king, possibly named Sil, is buried beneath the mound, sitting upright on a horse clothed, like its rider, in gold. Needless to say, such a story has prompted more than one attempt to uncover this tomb and its treasure, but none has succeeded. The most recent dig, carried out under the auspices of the BBC in 1968, failed to find anything conclusive, although its findings gave a more accurate picture than hitherto of the hill's construction and actual date.

Other local legends describe the hill as being built while a posset of milk was boiling, or by the Devil dropping clods from his spade while in the process of making Wansdyke. A variant of this tells that the Devil was on his way to Avebury when he met a man carrying a sack of shoes. He asked how far it was to the village and the man, who was a cobbler, told him he had worn out all the shoes just walking from there! The Devil promptly dumped his spadeful of earth on the spot, which became Silbury Hill. Michael Dames, in his book *The Silbury Treasure* (Thames and Hudson, 1976) put forward the persuasive theory that the hill, together with the ditch which surrounds it, form part of a monumental earth sculpture, depicting the goddess of the land in squatting position about to give birth. The hill is her womb, and the reflection of sun and moon on the water which at the time surrounded the mound, completed the imagery of the goddess giving birth to the Divine Child, probably at Lammas.

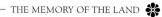

Thor's Cave

Staffordshire, OS SK 1055

THOR'S CAVE, also called Nan Tor, Wetton Mill and Thurshole, is situated in a wide valley where the Hoo Brook flows into the River Manifold. It was identified in the 1950s as a possible site of the Green Chapel, home of the fearsome Green Knight in the medieval poem *Sir Gawain and the Green Knight*. Local tradition also knows it as the Fiend's Hole, and together with its other names this suggests that there is an ancient association of the cave with a monster or demon of some kind. Whether this is the Devil or the Norse god Thor, or the enchanted spirit of winter known as the Green Knight remains uncertain, but the cave is certainly an eerie place. The discovery of bone tools and an axe-head in the cave itself suggests that it was probably home to a group of palaeolithic hunters, and it may well be that at one time a painting of some creature existed on one of the walls within, giving rise to the belief that a 'beast' lived within. Local tradition would have done the rest, supplying a name and face to the inhabitant of the cave.

Royston Cave

Hertfordshire, OS TL 357404

THIS IS undoubtedly one of the most fascinating sites in the whole of Britain, containing as it does much that is both enigmatic and mysterious. Accidentally rediscovered by a workman in 1742, the cave now lies beneath the A505 in the centre of the quiet town of Royston. The cave is roughly bell shaped, about 8.5 m (28 ft) deep, and is reached by a tunnel and

steps cut into the rock in the nineteenth century. The cave was found to be empty when it was opened up, but the walls are covered, from a little above floor level to a height of approximately 1.8 m (6 ft) with a mass of curious carvings. The imagery is extraordinary, and mixes pagan and Christian symbols in a wild confusion. Suggestions have been made that the military order of Knights Templar (condemned as heretics in the thirteenth century) may have used the cave, which possibly originated as a chalk pit or 'dene' dug by either Roman or Saxon farmers in the area. Among the recognizable carvings on the walls are a possible St Christopher, a possible St Catherine (though these could equally well be Cernunnos or Arianrhod), all interspersed with knights, crosses and a plethora of swords. As well as the Templars, a Rosicrucian connection has been invoked, deriving from the fact that earlier names for Royston are Crux Roies (1120), Croyrois (1263) and Villa de Cruce Rosia (1298). Local tradition speaks of a certain Lady Roese, whom at least one commentator has derived from Fair Rosamond, the mistress of Henry II, or *Rosa Mundi* (the Rose of the World), a title applied to the Virgin Mary in Christian iconography. Whatever the origin and use of Royston, the cave continues to fascinate, and if one stands within its dim, always cool recess, one cannot fail to be struck by the power of the carvings.

The Eildon Hills

Scotland, OS NT 555329 & 548027

HERE, ACCORDING to long standing tradition, the seer Thomas the Rhymer (Thomas of Erceldoune) met the Queen of Faery and went with her into the Otherworld. He remained there for three years, though it seemed only three days to him, and when he at last emerged he could no longer tell a lie and had acquired the gift of prophecy. His prophecies, written as a series of brief gnomic poems, still exist. Sir Walter Scott, who lived within the shadow of the hills, was so fond of the story that he loved to point out the original Eildon tree under which Thomas lay when he saw the Queen of Faery riding by. Today, a stone stands on the slope of the hills above the Boggle Burn, supposedly marking the spot where the tree once stood.

Apart from 'True Thomas' – as he was afterwards known – the hills are home to a whole series of famous personages. King Arthur is thought to lie beneath an Iron-Age hill-fort and cairns in an enchanted sleep, awaiting the call to awaken in time of his country's need. The same area is said to be so full of gold that the teeth of sheep who crop the grass there turn yellow! Michael Scott, the celebrated Scottish wizard, also has a connection with the Eildon Hills. It was he who transformed a single hill into three – setting this task to one of his demons as a test. Eildon Hill North (NT 5532) was used as signal station by the Romans, who built a large fortress to the east of Newstead (NT 5634), calling it Trimontium (Three Hills). It was the centre for Roman attempts to invade and control Scotland from AD 81.

Aberfoyle Faery Hill

Scotland, OS NN 5200

SCOTLAND ABOUNDS in faery hills, gateways between the worlds by which those fortunate – or unfortunate – enough to encounter their mysterious denizens could find their way into faeryland. One of the most famous is this hill at Aberfoyle, near Callander, in Perthshire. The vicar of Aberfoyle in the late 1600s was the Reverend Robert Kirk. He was also the author of one of the best surveys of faery lore ever written, *The Secret Commonwealth of Elves, Fauns and Fairies* (not published until 1893). When he died, on 14 May 1692, while actually walking on the faery hill, it was widely believed that he had been spirited away by the faery people. Shortly after his death, Kirk is said to have appeared to a cousin and to have informed him that it

was still possible to rescue him from faeryland. Kirk had left behind a posthumous child and promised to appear at its christening. If his cousin could throw an iron knife over his apparition when it appeared, then he would be saved – iron being traditionally deadly to the faery folk. However, when Kirk duly made his appearance, all there, including the cousin, were so astonished and fearful that the knife was never thrown and the vicar of Aberfoyle was never seen again. This story may owe something to Kirk's successor, Reverend Patrick Grahaeme, although once one has walked on the faery hill one cannot help but feel that the account might be true. Strips of cloth called 'cloutis' are still hung on the trees around the hill as offerings to the kindly folk.

Robert Kirk's Grave

Scotland, OS NN 5201

THE GRAVE of the Reverend Robert Kirk (1644–92), left, lies in the churchyard of Kirkton, in the shadow of the faery hill of Aberfoyle where he is believed to have been taken into faeryland (see above). The grave is covered by a stone slab bearing a Latin inscription, erected by Kirk's surviving family.

Robin Hood's Butts

Somerset, OS ST 234126

ACTUALLY A series of round barrows dating from the Bronze Age, the 'Butts' have acquired a traditional association with the famous outlaw Robin Hood. According to local legend the hollows on the top of each barrow, in reality places where they have been opened and excavated in the past, were made by Robin and his mighty henchman Little John by tossing quoits to and from each other. This is really a variant of the tales of the many mythical giants whose stone-tossing activities account for a wide variety of huge boulders lying alone in the landscape. One of the barrows, believed to contain treasure, was opened some time in the eighteenth century, but each night the earth that had been removed during the day was put back and after a while the diggers gave up. Whatever other bones they may have contained, the barrows became the burial-place for hundreds of Oliver Cromwell's Roundhead soldiers, killed in a battle that took place nearby.

Robin Hood's Stride

Derbyshire, OS SK 225625

THIS DRAMATIC natural outcrop rising from the middle of Harthill Moor is one of many sites that have attracted to themselves the name of Robin Hood. In much the same way as the numerous places that bear the name of King Arthur, these often have nothing to do with the bold outlaw of Sherwood. Here, the two pillar-like stones that top the cliff are said to have measured Robin's stride. In fact the alignment of the stones, which were measured by the writer John Barnatt in his book *Stone Circles of the Peak* (Turnstone Books, 1978), probably had something to do with the setting up of the adjacent Nine Stone Close, a circle of nine standing stones (only four now remain), which are aligned both to the Stride and to other significant points around the area, as well as to the rising and setting of both sun and moon over the moor and the surrounding hills.

The Stiperstones

Shropshire, OS SQ 3699

THESE HUGE boulders, which lie scattered along the back-bone of a rocky rise near the border between England and Wales, are believed to have been dropped there by the Devil as he rested there on his way from Ireland with an apron-ful of stones. The largest of the stones is called the Devil's Chair and has the usual story told of it that if anyone can spend a night in it he or she will be either mad or inspired by the morning. Another version of the tale says that there was a prophecy which related that England would fall into ruins when the Stiperstones sank into the ground. The Devil, hearing of this, sat in his chair and tried to push the stones into the earth. He failed, and England survived! A third story tells that as the Devil was passing one day he saw a giantess trying to carry off his chair. In anger, he cut her apron strings and the stones fell to earth, where they now lie.

A single stone, known as the Needle's Eye, stands further off on the hillside, and it is said that those brave enough to look through the hole which pierces it will actually catch a glimpse of the Devil going about his work! So strong is the association of devilish activity with the stones that local people swore they could still smell sulphur around the stones as recently as the nineteenth century.

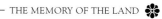

Hawkstone Park Monument

Shropshire, OS SJ 6136

THIS CURIOUS tower is a reconstruction of a much earlier monument that stood on the same site from 1795 until it fell victim to a violent storm in 1935. It was erected to the memory of Sir Rowland Hill, a much-loved and respected landowner who built on the remarkable site known as Hawkstone Park (see pages 110–11). A gentle and kindly man, Hill became the first Protestant Lord Mayor of London in 1594. (The statue that tops the tower shows Sir Rowland in his robes of office.) He was also listed among the many debtors of King Henry VIII who forbore to press the king for repayment in 1536 when the royal coffers were empty.

Kenfig Pool

Wales, OS SS 7981

AT ONE TIME there was an important Norman castle and township at Kenfig, which lies near to present-day Porthcawl. Over the years, sand engulfed the place, and it was gradually deserted. Local legend, however, records another story. In this, a local chieftain slew a certain prince, who with his dying breath laid a curse on the chieftain and his family for many generations. Long years after a cry was heard issuing from the earth itself: *'Dial a ddaw! Dial a ddaw!'* ('Vengeance is coming!') The chieftain of the time summoned his bard, who related the tale to him. But the chieftain scorned to believe the warning and instead ordered a feast to be held. In the midst of the celebrations the cry was heard again, and water burst into the hall, overwhelming the castle and inundating the village. No one escaped and from that moment Kenfig became a haunted spot.

In the nineteenth century traces of ruined masonry could still be seen beneath the water. An alternate version of the story relates how a poor peasant's son killed a local man and stole his money so that he could marry the local chieftain's daughter. During the wedding ceremony the voice cried out for vengeance and the inundation swiftly followed.

Pistyll-y-Rhaeadr

Wales, OS SN 9668

THE LARGEST waterfall in Wales, Pistyll-y-Rhaeadr cascades for some 73 m (240 ft) over rocks polished smooth by its descent. As so often with sites of this kind, there is a local legend that attributes it to the Devil, who is said to have split the rocks over which the water now gushes forth. Another local legend mentions the presence of a dragon in the area, who is likened in some way to the falls. It was finally killed when the people of nearby Llanrhaeadr yn Mochant constructed a pillar studded all over with iron spikes. The dragon was then lured to the place by the draping of the pillar with scarlet cloth, which attracted it in the same way that light attracts moths. The great beast beat itself to death against the spikes.

Owein Glyndwr's Footprint

Wales, OS SJ 0743

G LYNDWR (*c.* 1359–*c.* 1416) is one of the greatest heroes of Wales. In 1400 he took up arms after a dispute with his English neighbour Reginald Gray, Lord of Ruthin, who claimed a piece of land supposedly owned by Owein. From here the war extended as disaffected men flocked to Glyndwr's banner. In 1401 he was proclaimed Prince of Wales by his followers. Thereafter the rising spread until Owein won the support of the powerful Percy family of Northumberland and, shortly after that, of the Mortimers when Edmund Mortimer married Owein's daughter. By 1405 he had taken the castles of Harlech and Aberystwyth and afterwards received a large grant of lands in England – the extent and placing of which was determined according to bardic prophecy, which claimed Owein's descent from the rulers of Powys and Gwynedd. Owein's meteoric rise continued until 1406 when the forces of the English King Henry IV recaptured Harlech and Aberystwyth. With this the rising was effectively over, but Owein himself escaped and in the way of heroes vanished utterly. His whereabouts and death remain unrecorded, though a contemporary account records that he:

> . . . *went into hiding on St Matthew's Day in Harvest, and thereafter his hiding place was unknown. Very many say that he died; the seers maintain that he did not.*

Whatever the truth an aura of myth and strangeness gathered around the memory of the vanished Glyndwr, and he is remembered in a number of places around Corwyn. The 'footprint', supposedly left by him, is close to Glyndwr's Mount, the site of his manor-house. Glyndwr's Seat, which overlooks the town from the hill of Pen-y-Pigyn, recalls another local tradition. From there, Owein threw his dagger at the stone that now forms the lintel over the door of Corwyn's Church. The impression of a dagger may still be seen, though it was certainly carved there much earlier than Owein's time.

Penhale Sands

Cornwall, OS SW 768564

THE LONG reach of Penhale Sands, which lies adjacent to the coastal town of Perranporth, is said to cover an entire town, swallowed up as a punishment for the wickedness of its people. Although this is generally believed to be no more than a story, the remains of an ancient hermitage were uncovered there in 1835. The church was said to have been founded by St Piran, who is the patron saint of Cornish tin miners. Legend has it that he was thrown off a cliff in Ireland, chained to a millstone, as a punishment for preaching Christianity. However, the millstone floated and Piran was later washed up on the shores of Cornwall. His cult flourished there, and later spread to both Wales and Brittany. The site of his hermitage is marked by an ancient and much-weathered stone cross.

Above:
*A lonely Celtic cross
marks the spot where
an ancient hermitage
is believed to have
stood.*

Craig-y-Ddinas

Wales, OS SN 912080

SET AMID the splendours of the Vale of Neath just east of Pontneddfechan, this dramatic outcrop of rock is celebrated as one of the last bastions of the faery people in Wales. It is also one of the many sites where King Arthur and his knights lie sleeping in a cave below the hill, surrounded by treasure, and waiting for the day when they will be recalled to help their country in time of need. A story, told in variant forms at a number of sites, describes a local man who is shown the whereabouts of a cave by a magician, who tells him that if he accidentally touches a certain bell he will awaken one of the knights and, when asked if it is time to come forth, he must reply: 'No, sleep on.' On the first occasion this happens and the man remembers the correct answer, but when greed takes him once again into the cave and when he once again rings the bell, this time he cannot remember the correct formula, and is soundly beaten by the knight. An alternate story makes the sleeper the Welsh hero Owen Lawgoch, but the outcome is the same. There is in fact a system of caves called Will's Hole, which run beneath Craig-y-Ddinas, but these have never been fully explored, and so far no one has reported seeing the sleepers or finding the treasure!

Llyn Ddinas

Wales, OS SH 6149

OMEWHERE IN this area – local legend says beneath the lake – the tyrant Vortigern hid the throne of Britain. Vortigern is generally slated as the chieftain responsible for inviting the Saxons into Britain (they came as mercenaries but quickly became invaders) and for attempting to build a tower that would not stand at Dinas Emrys (see page 109). This brought him into contact with the young Merlin, and soon after he met his end, consumed by fire in his hall. It is unlikely that there ever was an actual throne of Britain, as there was no overall king at the time; but the story persists, and it would certainly have been in keeping with Vortigern's shifty disposition to hide the throne from anyone who came after him. The lakeside is also said to be the site of a battle between the Arthurian hero Owein and a giant. Merlin's treasure is also thought to be buried nearby.

Trereen Dinas

Cornwall, OS SW 432387

PERCHED ON the edge of Gurnard's Head, a long promontory that thrusts out into the sea near Zennor, is Trereen Dinas, an Iron-Age hill-fort which local tradition describes as belonging to a giant. The key to the castle was kept in a holed rock called the Giant's Lock, which lies below the fortress near the foot of the cliffs. King Arthur is also said to have used the site as a base for a campaign against the invading Danes. Further along the coast, towards Zennor, the story is told of Arthur having dined with four kings before going into battle.

CHAPTER FOUR

FORTRESSES OF CHIVALRY

MEDIEVAL CASTLES AND HALLS

DUNCAN: This castle hath a pleasant seat; the air
Nimbly and sweetly recommends itself
Unto our gentle senses.
BANQUO: This guest of summer,
The temple-haunting martlet, does approve
By his lov'd mansionry that the heaven's breath
Smells wooingly here. No jutty, frieze,
Buttress, nor coign of vantage, but this bird
Hath made his pendent bed and procreant cradle.

William Shakespeare, *Macbeth*

IF THE LAND itself can be said to remember its past, then the stone buildings placed upon it are just as full of memories. Castles and towers, halls and chambers have their own tales to tell. Arundel Castle in Sussex (see pages 98–9) still houses the sword which is said to have belonged to the giant Bevis of Hampton, remembered in the medieval romance of that name as a hero who, having been sold into slavery, escaped to survive many more adventures with the help of his magical sword Morglay (given him by the daughter of the King of Armenia) and his horse Arundel – which is possibly the only reason why his story is in fact associated with that great medieval castle.

Tintagel, long believed to be the birthplace of King Arthur, and Pendragon Castle, perhaps the home of his father Uther Pendragon, have well-established histories associating them with these figures. Other buildings, such as Richmond Castle, Sheriff Hutton and Skipton, all bear witness to the colourful history of the Middle Ages, a time of terrible suffering for the peasants of Britain, and a time of military might and vaunting chivalry for the nobility who ruled the land with blood and brawn. But it is not always the true tales of history that we remember when we visit these places; often it is the glorious myths of brave knights and their fair ladies that draw us still to places like the Great Hall of Winchester (see page 106), where a medieval replica of the Round Table at which Arthur and his knights were believed to have sat still hangs on the wall, adorned not with a picture of the great British hero, but with a portrait of Henry VIII.

In London, at the Tower (see page 100), we once again meet the story of the palladium, the 'luck' of Britain, in the story of the head of Bran, buried there with its face towards France until it was dug up by Arthur himself. People remembered these stories, and told them again and again, adding details that made them more explicable to each passing generation. Thus the Celtic hero Arthur becomes a medieval king, and his rough-hewn band of heroes the steel-clad Knights of the Round Table.

Although there were probably never more than a few million people in the whole of medieval Britain, yet it is the buildings they constructed that still dominate the horizons in many of our towns and cities, where the steeples of medieval cathedrals and the massive walls of castles stand out amid modern houses and shops.

To the medieval mind memory of times past (which we now call history) was all of a piece, timeless, and like a seamless garment. Medieval people included Julius Caesar and Orpheus, the Minotaur and Arthur together, and gave a place on their maps to dragons and other monsters alongside the road to Paradise and the holy city of Jerusalem. As the historian Peter Vansittart puts it in his book *Green Knights, Black Angels* (Macmillan, 1969):

'History' was old tales and songs, expected to provide not precise information but poetic illustrations of moral order, heroic qualities, divine purpose, and the need for national unity. Much of it was invented by such excellent narrators as Geoffrey of Monmouth [The History of the Kings of Britain, c. 1136] *for those ends.*

Previous pages: The mighty bulk of St Michael's Mount dominates the shoreline of Mount's Bay, Cornwall.

It is these dreams and stories, these old tales and songs, which bring us back, time and again, to the castles and halls of medieval Britain, for they are really stone books waiting to tell us of the great days of chivalry and adventure, which are as much a part of the heritage that is legendary Britain as the dates and real events of history itself.

Arundel Castle

Sussex, OS TQ 0107

A RUNDEL CASTLE is one of the finest medieval buildings still standing, though much of it was restored in the eighteenth and nineteenth centuries. Built by Roger Montgomery, shortly after the Norman Conquest, it was added to in 1170 and 1190, and after the Wars of the Roses became the seat of the Duke of Norfolk. In the armoury rests a huge two-handed sword called Morglay, which tradition attributes to the great hero Bevis of Hampton (Southampton), who was so huge that he could walk through the sea from his home to Cowes without getting his head wet. According to tradition, Bevis served for many years as the warden of Arundel, and built himself a massive tower in which he could live. A seventeenth-century translator of Camden's *Britannia* comments:

> For that Bevis was founder of the castle is a current opinion handed on by tradition; and there is a tower in it still, known by the name of Bevis's tower, which they say was his own apartment.

However, the association probably comes from the fact that the hero's horse was called Arundel, though it has been suggested that the castle was named after the hero's horse rather than the other way around. The story is also told that when Bevis felt his life was drawing to a close, he threw his sword from the battlements of the castle. It landed 750 m (½ mile) away on a mound still called Bevis's Grave, which is in fact an ancient long barrow (recently destroyed); this may even have been the beginning of the story of a Sussex giant living in that area. Bevis's adventures are told in a fourteenth-century story *Bevis of Hamptoun*.

The White Tower

London, OS TQ 3380

THE TOWER of London has probably seen more history than almost any other site in the country. Built by William the Conqueror and added to by successive owners, the tower's legendary history rests on one particular story found in the great collection of Celtic myth lore known as *The Mabinogion*. The story tells how Bran the Blessed, wounded in warfare against the Irish, commanded his followers to cut off his head and carry it to London, where it was to be buried beneath the hill known as the White Mount with its face towards France. As long as it remained there, the story went, no enemy would ever succeed in conquering Britain. According to a later tradition it was King Arthur who commanded the head to be disinterred,

> *. . . since he did not desire that this island should be guarded by anyone's strength but his own.*
>
> (*The Welsh Triads*)

The White Mount is generally believed to be the hill on which the Conqueror's tower was built, and indeed some writers have suggested that it got its name from the fact that the tower was whitewashed on the outside. However, the Celtic tradition is older than this. It may derive from the fact that the word for white in Welsh can also mean holy, suggesting that an older stratum of legend is being drawn upon. Since the legendary founder of Britain, the Trojan Brutus, is also said to have been buried in the White Mount, this may also add to the story, and it may also be the case that a temple to the sacred head, which had magical status among the Celts, may have been here before any

of the stories were told. To this day ravens are kept at the Tower, and their wings are clipped to prevent them flying away since, according to tradition, bad luck will ensue if the ravens depart. The fact that the name Bran also means 'raven' may have something to do with this, despite the fact that the ravens are only believed to have been introduced into the Tower by Charles II in the seventeenth century.

Tintagel Castle

Cornwall, OS SX 050890

Right:
Tintagel Castle, the possible birthplace of King Arthur.

Below:
The White Tower, said to have been the burial place of the head of the Celtic god, Bran.

THESE DRAMATIC ruins, perched on the cliffs above the Atlantic, are all that remain of a once mighty Norman castle, begun in 1140 by Reginald, Earl of Cornwall, and added to over the next 300 years by successive owners. However, it is not these mundane facts that have made Tintagel famous, but its association with King Arthur, whose reputed birthplace it is. In fact, there is little to support the story, which first appears in the writings of the medieval chronicler Geoffrey of Monmouth in the twelfth century. Arthur, if he lived at all, existed long before there was a castle on the headland, though there was a flourishing monastic community, founded by St Juliot, which is roughly contemporary with the hero's dates (sixth century AD).

The recent discovery of a larger, secular community, and a stone bearing a footprint, suggests that there may be more to the legend than has been previously acknowledged. The possibility that Arthur may indeed have lived for a time at Tintagel has at least a basis in archaeological fact – though no precise documentation has ever been discovered to support these claims. The other story, relating to the discovery of the child Arthur on the shore by Merlin's Cave, dates back no further than Tennyson's Victorian poems, *Idylls of the King*.

Pendragon Castle

Cumbria, OS NY 782026

LITTLE NOW remains of this once imposing Norman castle, dating from the eleventh century but probably built upon the site of an earlier fortress. Its name, Pendragon Castle, explains its association with Arthur. His father was named Uther Pendragon and Arthur himself bore this same title. For title it is, meaning 'Chief Dragon', or possibly 'Dragon Head', which has been taken as a reference to the dragon standard born by the hero in many of the earliest accounts of his deeds. There is a brief mention of the castle in Malory's celebrated book *Le Morte d'Arthur* (1485), where a castle bearing this name is given as a gift by Sir Lancelot to a young knight named Brunor le Noir.

St Michael's Mount

Cornwall, OS SW 514298

THE DRAMATIC bulk of St Michael's Mount, rising from the sands of Mount's Bay, are recorded in a twelfth-century romance as being the place where the hermit Ogrin, who had given shelter to the runaway lovers Tristan and Iseult, went to buy some fine clothes for Iseult to wear when she attempted to return to her estranged husband King Mark of Cornwall. Another story, which relates how King Arthur slew the giant of Mont St Michel in France, may relate to the Cornish sites as there are legends that tell of a giant named Cormoran living in the area.

Nowadays the site is among the most romantic and powerful in the area. From the top of the steeply climbing steps that wind around the cliffs, the views across to the mainland are worth every bit of the effort required to reach them.

Opposite:
At low tide a causeway stretches across to the normally seabound mass of St Michael's Mount.

The Great Hall, Winchester

Hampshire, OS SU 478295

SIR THOMAS MALORY, in his great epic of Arthurian romance stated unequivocally that Winchester was Camelot, Arthur's chief city and the setting of many of the most memorable events in the story. Here Arthur and Guinevere were married and here, 40 years or so later, the king prepared to burn his wife for her adultery with Lancelot. The main reason for the association is almost certainly the 'Round Table' which hangs in the Great Hall, all that remains of a twelfth-century castle. The table dates from perhaps as early as the twelfth or thirteenth centuries, but is no older. It may have been commissioned by Edward I (1239–1307), an Arthurian enthusiast. It currently bears a picture of Henry VIII as Arthur, a painting commissioned by the king in 1522 to impress a visiting monarch. Before the table, or the hall, were built, Winchester was the capital of Saxon England. Before that, it was a Roman city, Venta Belgarum.

Richmond Castle

Yorkshire, OS NZ 171007

LOCAL TRADITION tells that beneath the massive rocks on which Richmond Castle sits lie the bodies of King Arthur and his knights – not dead but sleeping, awaiting the day when their country's need will recall them to wakefulness. A story tells that a potter named Thompson once found his way by accident into the cave beneath the hill and found himself in a cavern where the knights lay sleeping. On a table in the centre were a sword in its sheath and a great horn. Terrified by what he saw Thomson fled, and as he did so heard the words:

Potter Thompson, Potter Thompson
If thou hadst either drawn
The sword or blown the horn,
Thou'd been the luckiest man
That ever yet was born!

This is probably no more than another of the many stories that tell of Arthur's enchanted sleep – itself a memory of earlier beliefs that the soul of the king is bound to the land. Yet a map, dating from 1610, shows the entrance to a tunnel south of the town of Richmond itself, next to the fast-flowing River Swale. The notation next to this reads:

This passage is one that goeth under the river and ascendeth up into the castle.

No trace of this passage has ever been found, however, any more than the reputed cavern, though many have sought the treasure believed to lie there with the king and his men.

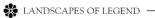

Dinas Emrys

Wales, OS SH 606492

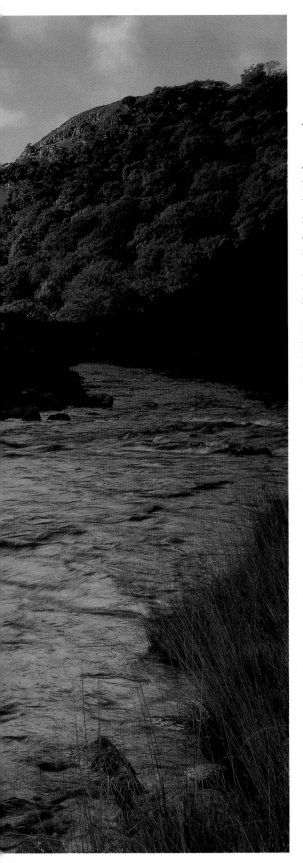

HERE, ON TOP of this impressive bulk of a hill near the town of Bangor, legend recalls that the tyrant Vortigern attempted to build a tower. When the work carried out by his masons fell down in the night Vortigern demanded of his Druids the cause and the cure. They told him that he must find a child without a father and sacrifice him, pouring out his blood on the foundations. Vortigern sent out his soldiers to search for such a child and they returned with a youth named Myrddin Emrys, the future Merlin of King Arthur's court. The child proceeded to confound the Druids by telling them that the real reason for the scattering of the walls was that two dragons lived beneath the hill and awoke to fight every night. A pit was subsequently dug, and Merlin was proved correct in every detail. He then made a series of prophecies, including the death of Vortigern, the coming of Arthur, and the eventual end of time. Today the ruins which crown the hill are medieval, though archaeological evidence suggests that it was fortified some time in the sixth century, when Arthur is believed to have flourished. It offers spectacular views of Mount Snowdon (see pages 44–5) and of the wild valley of the River Glaswyn below.

Hawkstone Park

Shropshire, OS SJ 6136

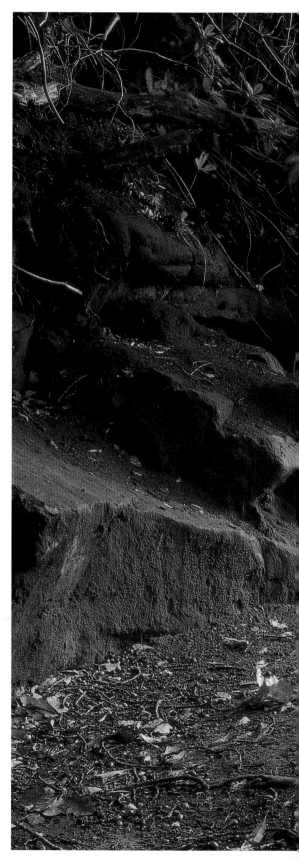

HAWKSTONE IS a remarkable site in every way, containing evidence of occupation from the Stone Age onwards. The remains of a medieval fortress, called the Red Castle, stand on the steep natural outcrop known as Redcliff. This was probably built by a member of the Audley family, Henry de Audley, who served as Sheriff of Shropshire from 1216 to 1221. It remained in the family for a number of generations, until it passed into the hands of Sir Rowland Hill in 1737. A local tradition tells of two huge knights, Sir Tarquin and Sir Tarquinus, who possessed the castle in Arthurian times. These characters both appear in Malory's *Le Morte d'Arthur,* and one of them – Tarquin – wears red armour. Another story, related in a nineteenth-century account of the history of Hawkstone, tells how Sir Edward and Sir Hue of the Red Castle disinherited the Lady of the Rock, who appealed to the great Round Table knight Sir Ewain for help. He was glad to assist and soon ransomed the lady's lands for her. It is interesting that the name of this knight derives from an earlier, Celtic hero named Owein, thus suggesting a more ancient history for this story.

Sheriff Hutton Castle

Yorkshire, OS SE 6566

THIS ONCE powerful castle saw many dramatic events, and one great mystery, during the reign of Richard III (1452–85). Here, in 1482, Anthony Woodville, Earl Rivers, was informed that, because of the plot engineered by his sister, the Queen, against Richard, he was to be executed. Given paper and pen he wrote his will – and also a poem filled with the anguish of a tortured soul:

> Somewhat musing,
> And more mourning,
> In remembering
>   Th'unsteadfastness;
> This world being
> Of such wheeling,
> Me contrarying,
>   What may I guess?

A year later, evidence suggests that Richard may have sent the two young princes – now declared bastards – Edward, the son of King Edward IV, and Richard, Duke of York, together better known as the 'Princes in the Tower', to Sheriff Hutton. Despite the continuing tradition that the children were smothered while held prisoner in the tower, there is no final proof that this event ever took place. Household records of Sheriff Hutton make brief mention of provisions being made for two unnamed 'guests', who may indeed have been the two princes, smuggled out of London even while word of their deaths was beginning to spread. Whether they later died in this castle or were taken elsewhere will probably never be known.

Skipton Castle

Yorkshire, OS SD 9851

IN SHARP contrast to the memorials of the industrial age that surround it, the rugged walls of Skipton Castle (opposite) still loom large over the town which bears its name. Seat of the great Clifford family, it dates mostly from the fourteenth to seventeenth centuries, though the remains of a Norman gatehouse built by Robert de Romille still stands. A remarkable room, lined with seashells, exists alongside the dungeon, which is believed to be haunted by the ghosts of prisoners held there during the fifteenth century.

Helmsley Castle

Yorkshire, OS SE 6183

NOT FAR from the Roman road that crosses Wheeldale Moor (see page 54) lies the ruined bulk of Helmsley Castle, built by Walter l'Espec, who founded the mighty Rievaulx Abbey two miles to the north-west of the castle. The great twelfth-century fortress received a battering from the cannon of Cromwell's forces during a three-month-long siege. It fell into ruins after it was bought in 1689 by Sir Charles Duncome, who then built a manor-house in the grounds and allowed the castle to fall victim to wind and weather.

CHAPTER FIVE

CELEBRATIONS IN STONE

FROM TOMB TO CATHEDRAL

. . . and many, many more whose names are
. . . on the diptycha of the Island
. . . whether men or womenkind,
. . . whether bond or free . . . of far back
or of but recent decease, whose burial
mounds are known or unknown
or for whom no mound was ever raised
or any mark set up of even the meanest
sort to show the site of their interment.

David Jones, *The Sleeping Lord*

WE HAVE lost a great deal in our movement from village life to urban community. A sense of the significance of place, of the continuity of history, as well as of individual values. More, we have begun to lose the stories we once told each other, the mythology of heath and hedgerow, tumulus and track, which were constant memorials to a time that was past but which remained part of our consciousness. Thankfully, many of these stories were preserved, at least in part, by the dedicated folklorists and antiquaries of the nineteenth century. In recent times we have begun to see a re-emergence of interest in the history of the land itself, along with some reappraisal of the imperfectly understood rituals that still lie embedded in the countryside itself.

The existence of these legendary presences within the land, whether it be in places like Wayland's Smithy (see pages 122–3) where the smith of the gods may still shoe your horse for the gift of a coin, or the mysterious carvings at Maes Howe in the Orkneys (see page 132), adds a patina of wonder to hill and valley, earth and stone alike. Even the mighty cathedrals of the Middle Ages have their share of legend and story, and as often as not stand upon the foundations of older sanctuaries.

The land itself thus becomes an extraordinary palimpsest, with layer upon layer of history, legends and stories lying just below the surface. The very age of the places gives them a curious feeling of having always been there. As Jacquetta Hawkes wrote in her wonderful evocation of the landscape, which she called simply *A Land* (The Cresset Press, 1951):

Previous pages:
The mysterious
Lake Bala, Wales.

It is this immense antiquity that gives our land its look of confidence and peace, its power to give us both rest and inspiration. When returning from hill or moor one looks down on a village . . . swaddled in trees, and with only the church tower breaking the thin blue layer of evening smoke, the emotion it provokes is as precious as it may be commonplace. Time, that has caressed this place until it lies as comfortably as a favourite cat in an armchair, caresses also even the least imaginative of beholders.

One hardly needs to be imaginative when one stands by the side of the worn cluster of stones traditionally believed to be the resting-place of the great Celtic bard Taliesin. He it was who wrote of an even deeper identification with all of creation:

I have been in many shapes
before I assumed a constant form:
I have been a narrow sword,
A drop in the air,
A shining bright star,
A letter among words
In the book of origins.

The overlapping layers of history are remembered again and again in the places pictured here. The Clava cairns (see pages 128–9) near Croy in Scotland, recall the ritual interment of countless generations; while Kilpeck Church in Herefordshire bears inscribed on its walls symbols that recall several ages of belief – not all of them Christian.

It is these things which are the memorials not only of history but of a legendary past, a past that informs our lives and that is part of the living landscape through which we walk every day. Even if we never set foot outside the cities in which so many of us are forced to live, the presence of the legendary landscape is all around us, preserving the deeper mysteries of place and time, and ensuring that they are ultimately remembered for as long as the land itself continues to exist.

Bryn Celli Dhu

Wales, OS SH 508702

THIS IS one of the finest examples of a prehistoric burial mound in Britain. In fact it is really a chambered tomb built upon an earlier henge monument. During excavations carried out at the site in the 1950s large numbers of bones, both burned and unburned, were discovered, bearing testimony to the use of the site over a long period of time. Local legend describes it as a dwelling-place of the spirits, and much has been written about the curious carvings inscribed on one side of the central standing stone outside the entrance. Inside the chamber is a central stone, which has a whitish colour to it. According to a local historian, this was initially taken for a carved figure when the tomb was opened in the late 1900s. The name of the site means 'The Hill in the Dark Grove' suggesting that there may at one time have been a sacred enclosure of trees around it.

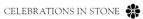

Wayland's Smithy

Oxfordshire, OS SU 281854

L YING JUST off the great neolithic track of the Ridgeway, Wayland's Smithy is believed to be the home of a mysterious blacksmith described by the seventeenth-century antiquary Francis Wise as:

> *. . . an invisible smith . . .* [of whom it was said that] *if a traveller's horse had lost a shoe upon the road, he had no more to do than to bring the horse to this place with a piece of money, and leaving both there for some little time, he might come again and find the money gone, but the horse new shod.*

This tradition dates back well into the eighteenth century, and probably derives from a much earlier story. Wayland is a corruption of the Norse Volund, a magical smith whose skill was such that he came to the attention of King Nidudr, who captured and lamed him so that he might not escape. But Volund took a terrible revenge. He lured the king's two sons to his smithy and, having killed them, made drinking vessels from their skulls which he then sent to the king. The story is recorded more than once in old English poems, including the tenth-century *Deor*. It also appears, in pictographic terms, on an ancient casket believed to have been carved out of whalebone in the eighth century. How far back the story can be traced in its present form is uncertain. The site actually consists of a megalithic tomb built on top of an older barrow dating from around 3600 BC. The name Welandes Smidde appears in a charter of the ninth century, and on a map dated 1828 it is still called Wayland Smith's forge. Its close proximity to the Uffington White Horse (see pages 40–1) has led to the suggestion that this had something to do with the origin of the story, but there is no proof of this.

Bedd Taliesin

Wales, OS SN 672912

TALIESIN, THE great sixth-century mystical poet who is later supposed to have become the court poet of King Arthur, is believed to be buried here, on the slopes of Moel-y-Garn. A local belief says that anyone who spends the night amid the tumbled rocks of the cairn (all that remain after centuries of pillaging by local farmers) will awaken either mad or a poet. Another tale describes how, in the nineteenth century, a number of well-intentioned antiquarians searched the grave for the bones of Taliesin, intending to re-inter them in another spot. As they dug, however, a fearsome storm began, lightning crashed and thunder rolled. The men, fearful of disturbing the poet's rest, ran away, never to return. The grave is probably the remains of a cist-type burial that did indeed contain bones – though what happened to them or where they went is unknown. Taliesin's legend is described in *The Mabinogion*, where he is the offspring of a divine birth from the goddess Ceridwen. Able to speak poetry from birth, he left a puzzling collection of poems – not all of them necessarily by him, which contain evidence of the continued practice of shamanism in Britain at least as late as the sixth century.

Lake Bala

Wales, OS SH 9033

THE LARGEST stretch of natural water in Wales, Llyn Tegid (Bala Lake) got its name from Tegid Foel, a fifth-century nobleman who ruled over the surrounding area. His wife was Ceridwen, mother of the great bard and poet Taliesin (see page 124) whose efforts to make her hideously ugly son Afagddu clever resulted in Taliesin imbibing the magical drink that she had brewed. Taliesin thereafter became the wisest man in the land and wrote a series of cunningly devised poems, which are still hard to understand today. Local tradition records that the original town of Bala was drowned beneath the lake at some time in the distant past. A number of reasons are given, one being that the cover was accidentally left off the magical well of Ffynnon Gywer, which then overflowed, covering the town. Another story is identical to that told of Kenfig Pool in Cornwall (see page 83) where the wickedness of the inhabitants caused the waters to rise and drown them all. The lake was widely believed to be bottomless, and when a man went out to what was said to be the deepest spot and threw a plumbline over the side of his boat, he heard a voice cry out 'Line cannot fathom me. Go, or I shall swallow you up!' In more recent times a diver went down into the lake and reported seeing a dragon coiled on the bottom. Other stories of a mysterious humpbacked beast arising from the waters have begun to rival sightings of 'Nessie' in Scotland's Loch Ness. Certainly the place has a slightly sinister air about it, especially on a dull or overcast day.

Clava Cairns

Scotland, OS NH 7644

THE PROPER name for this remarkable site is Balnuaran of Clava. It consists of three 'clava' or ring cairns, each of which is contained within a stone circle. They date from the late Stone Age, which has not prevented them from being described as 'Druid' circles by those who saw only the fragmentary walls which were left standing from the seventeenth century onwards. Dr Johnson, accompanied by his faithful scribe James Boswell, visited the site in 1773. Johnson's acerbic comment was to the effect that:

to go and see one druidical temple is only to see that it is nothing, for there is neither art nor power in it; and seeing one is quite enough.

At one time the structures would have had corbelled roofs, while the central chambered tomb also possesses a cist containing funerary remains. The presence of stones bearing 'cup and ring' marks (small patterns of circles and indentations carved into the stones) strengthens the ritual significance of the site, since these markings have generally to do with alignments towards sun and moon – in this case perhaps relating to the passage of the soul to the Otherworld. Two of the three entrance passageways which led into the cairns are also aligned with the midwinter sunset, which adds to this belief. Local tradition makes the Clava Cairns the burial-place of the great Pictish king, Brude.

West Kennet Long Barrow

Wiltshire, OS SU 104677

ONE OF the most impressive burial mounds belonging to the complex of sites around Avebury (see pages 22–3), the barrow has been dated to 2500 BC and was used intermittently as a tomb from that date until around 1500 BC, after which it seems to have become more specifically oriented towards other ritual purposes. The mound is made of chalk, faced with large stones. It measures 100 m (330 ft) – of which 12 m (40 ft) consists of the interior space – and is from 2.4 to 3 m (8 to 10 ft) high. It was excavated in the 1950s and evidence was found of burials in the separate chambers that lie to either side of the main passage. It appears that the site was deliberately blocked off some time in the distant past, either to keep the spirits contained within, or to prevent misuse of the sacred place. This did not deter a seventeenth-century physician, Dr R. Toppe, from digging into the mound in order to find human bones, which he then ground into powder and put in his medicines!

Maes Howe

Orkney Islands, OS HY 318127

MAES HOWE is among the best-preserved chamber tombs in the whole of Europe. Covered by grass, the mound is well over 7.5 m (25 ft) high and over 45.4 m (150 ft) in diameter. Within, the mound contains a square chamber over 45.4 m (15 ft) high, with a great corbelled roof that is a marvel of architecture and skill in construction. It was probably begun around 2700 BC and has weathered the test of time remarkably well. A narrow passage, some 5.4 m (18 ft) long, allows entrance to the central chamber, and the sun enters along this shaft at midwinter, lighting the chamber for a few brief moments. Although the chamber is said to have been primarily used for funerary rites, it seems hard to believe that such a huge and complex structure was not also used for some other kinds of ritual. The story of the discovery of 'treasure' (see opposite) by the Vikings in the tenth century may in fact refer not to prehistoric objects, but to items hidden by the Norsemen themselves and then taken away by a rival group.

Maes Howe Runic Slab

Orkney Islands, OS HY 318127

THE RUNIC slab, found within Maes Howe, offers something of a mystery. The inscriptions have been translated to read as follows:

> HAKON ALONE BORE THE TREASURE OUT OF THIS MOUND. IT IS CERTAIN AND TRUE AS I SAY, THAT THE TREASURE HAS BEEN MOVED FROM HERE. THE TREASURE WAS TAKEN AWAY THREE NIGHTS BEFORE THEY BROKE INTO THIS MOUND.

> THESE RUNES HAVE BEEN CARVED BY THE MAN MOST SKILLED IN RUNES IN THE WESTERN OCEAN WITH THE AXE THAT BELONGED TO GUKR TRANDILSSON IN THE SOUTH OF ICELAND.

This is curious. The insistence, and repetition of the fact that treasure had been removed from the mound before it was broken into is puzzling. According to an account in the tenth-century *Orkneyinga Saga*, a party of Viking warriors under the leadership of Earl Harald Maddadarson were forced to take shelter at Maes Howe during a storm. The text reports that in the morning two of the men were 'stark mad', though the reason is not given. Is it possible that some ancient guardian was awoken by the threat to the treasure and bones hidden within the howe (grave)? Local tradition relates that the mound was believed to be inhabited by the Hogboy, but this is merely a mistranslation of *haugbui*, Norse for ghost, a further recollection perhaps of a spirit set to watch over the tomb.

Knowlton Circles

Dorset, OS SU 024103

ONE OF the few surviving examples of a stone circle within which a Christian church has been built, probably as a very deliberate attempt to show how the later religion had overcome or replaced the former. Generally, as in so many recorded instances, such sites would have been very deliberately destroyed, so that it shows an unusually enlightened approach in preserving the original circle of stones more or less untouched. In fact, a letter exists from Pope Gregory VII (*c.* 1023–85) to one Abbot Mellitus, stating that pagan temples ought not to be destroyed but wherever possible sanctified and converted into churches. Knowlton is one of the few where this seems to have been done. The remains of the church date from the twelfth century or even earlier, while the circle itself dates from the early Bronze Age.

Kilpeck Church

Herefordshire, OS SO 445305

KILPECK DISPLAYS some of the most remarkable carving to be found anywhere in the country, which combine both Christian and pagan symbolism in a remarkable way. Around the arches that frame its doors are depicted zodiacal creatures, strange heads, half-human, half-animal, a phoenix in flames, and several dragons. Perhaps most unusual and justly famous is the *sheela-na-gig* – an Irish phrase for the depiction of a squatting woman baring her vulva, which may well hark back to the worship of the Great Goddess (in some local form) at a very early period of time. Indeed there are a number of such carved figures to be found, both inside and outside churches throughout Britain. Most are discreetly hidden: this is a rare example of such a carving in such a prominent place. The carvings draw upon Celtic, Norse and even older indigenous symbolism, binding all together into a remarkable chorus of styles. The present church dates from the twelfth century, but incorporates an earlier Anglo-Saxon structure.

Rosslyn Chapel

Scotland, OS NT 2663

A FEW MILES south of Edinburgh lies one of the strangest and most mysterious buildings in the country. Rosslyn Chapel was intended to be part of a much larger cathedral begun in 1446; building stopped in about 1488, when the Saint-Clair family, who had commissioned the building, ran out of money. Even so, the part of the building which was completed – essentially a chapel some 21 m (70 ft) by 10.6 m (35 ft) and rising to 12.4 m (41 ft) in height, is a remarkable combination of symbolism drawn from Templar, Rosicrucian, Freemasonic and Grail traditions, reflecting a deep and mysterious fascination of its builders with the esoteric. The building contains a riot of carvings, both within and without, which have been justly described as 'a fevered hallucination in stone' (Michael Baigent and Richard Leigh in *The Temple & the Lodge*, Jonathan Cape, 1989). These carvings, together with the Saint-Clair (or Sinclair) family, have recently come under close scrutiny by a number of researchers.

Among other mysteries are the possible early voyage of Earl Henry Sinclair from the Orkneys to the American mainland – a voyage carried out some 50 years before Columbus, which is possibly remembered by the carving, on one of the pillars, of a type of corn only found in the Americas. There are also references within the carvings to the Grail myths, which are also reflected in one of the most curious stories of Rosslyn. This concerns the construction of an extraordinary stone pillar, which depicts four dragons coiled around its base. From their mouths issue the stems of four double spirals of foliage that wind around the column, bound to it by carved ropes of stone. On the capitals of the pillar are carved reliefs depicting the sacrifice of Isaac, all executed with astonishing realism and power. The story that is told concerning this pillar tells how the master mason was summoned to Rome, and how, during his absence, his apprentice completed the work on the pillar. When the master returned, he was so incensed by the brilliance of his pupil's work that he seized a hammer and struck him dead. A depiction in stone of a bearded man, and of a youth with a head wound, are to be found above the west door of the chapel. Since this event the pillar is widely known as the 'prentice pillar', and a legend has grown up that no lesser prize than the Holy Grail itself is hidden within.

Recent work, carried out by the family, has produced some intriguing speculations concerning the contents of the extensive vaults beneath the chapel. These are filled with sand and are therefore almost impossible to excavate, but electronic soundings suggest the presence of more than one body, clad in armour, as well as other possible items of a more mysterious character. The jury is still out on the validity or otherwise of the claims made for Rosslyn's hidden treasures, but it remains one of the more intriguing sites in legendary Britain.

St Magnus Cathedral

Orkney Islands, OS HY 4410

THIS MAGNIFICENT cathedral is one of the finest examples of a twelfth-century ecclesiastical building to survive. Founded in 1137, it commemorates the life and death of one of Orkney's greatest heroes – Magnus Erlendsson. A peace-maker at heart, Magnus shared his earldom with the Viking Haakon Paulsson, who was as savage as Magnus was gentle. In 1117, advised by his councillors to meet with the Viking leader and to attempt to resolve their differences, the earl made his way to the previously arranged meeting place on the tiny islet of Egilsay; there he was treacherously murdered by his enemy. Stories of miracles claimed in his name soon multiplied, and within 20 years of his death Magnus was canonized. A tradition that his relics were hidden in one of the pillars of the cathedral proved true in 1919 when they were discovered and re-interred within the nave of the cathedral.

Wells Cathedral

Somerset, OS ST 552459

THE CATHEDRAL of Wells is one of the oldest Christian foundations in the country, tracing its origins back to AD 909. Archaeological investigations carried out in 1978 showed that an older Saxon church was hidden partly beneath the present building, and that this had been aligned with the ancient holy well of St Andrew. The present building, one of the finest in the Western world, was begun in 1180 and not completed in its present form until the fifteenth century. However, the crowning glory of the building must be the west façade, with its astonishing tracery of statues, carvings and decorations, once painted in startling colours that must have been visible for miles across the flat Somerset plains. Completed in 1282, the façade contains over 400 figures. Over the north door is depicted the strange tale of King Edmund of the East Angles, who was defeated by the Danes at Hoxne and beheaded when he refused to renounce his Christian beliefs. The Danes hid his severed head in some thick brambles, so that it could not be found and buried with his body. When his followers came in search of the dead king's corpse they began to search the woods, calling out to each other so that they did not get lost. They then heard the king's voice calling out and by following the direction of the voice found the head, guarded by a wolf. The animal allowed them to take the head and followed them all the way until they left the woods, then turned away after having seen to the safety of the relic. Within the next decade the king was acknowledged as a martyr.

St Winifred's Well, Holywell

Wales, OS SJ 1847

A REMARKABLE story is told of the foundation of Winifrid's Well. The seventh-century Winifrid, whose real name was Gwenfrewi, was at home one day when a local chieftain from Hearden, named Caradoc, came to see her father. Immediately enamoured of the young woman he attempted to rape her, but she fled from him. According to one version of the story, before he caught her she reached a nearby chapel where her uncle, St Bueno, was preaching. At this point Caradoc drew his sword and cut off Winifrid's head. In this version her body fell outside the chapel, while her head rolled inside. In another version she was killed on the hill overlooking the chapel, and her head rolled down and through the entrance. In both cases St Bueno at once demanded that God punish Caradoc, who simply melted away. The saint then replaced the severed head on the body and covered the corpse with his cloak. He continued preaching and by the time he had finished Winifred sprang up alive. Ever after she had a red ring around her neck where the sword had struck her, and where her head had fallen a well began to bubble forth. A suitable housing was made for it, and this grew in time into the sizeable foundation that stands on the site to this day. Water still bubbles from the well and pilgrims in search of healing visit the shrine, bathing first in a star-shaped inner pool before proceeding to an outer pool where they kneel on the stone known as Bueno's Stone. The American folklorist Wirt Sykes visited the site in 1880 and recorded that:

> *This well discharges twenty-tones of water per minute, feeds an artificial lake, runs a mill and has cured un-numbered thousands of human beings of their ills for hundreds of years. It is surely one of the wonders of the world, to which even mystical legend can only add one marvel more.*

The unfortunate descendants of Caradoc were said to bark like dogs – the result of St Bueno's curse, which could only be cured by complete immersion in the well. At the bottom of the well a fragrant moss, which bears a reddish tinge, grows. It is called St Winifrid's hair in memory of the Saint.

Hawkstone Grotto

Shropshire, OS SJ 6136

W E HAVE already seen something of the extensive site that is Hawkstone Park with its fine Red Castle and Arthurian legends (see pages 110–11). As well as the castle there exists a remarkable series of caves, facing the medieval stronghold from across the valley. These caves have been systematically enlarged and modified since the Middle Ages. At one time they were decorated with thousands of semi-precious stones, lovingly installed there by Sir Richard Hill around 1795. This became a favourite spot for Victorian travellers, who enjoyed wandering through the maze of caverns and hearing the stories of Arthurian heroes. On their way up to the hilltop they would have encountered the mysterious 'Hermit of Hawkstone', one Father Francis, who would deliver a brief sermon before sending them on their way. Today this is recalled by a rather strange and garish model that comes to life at the touch of a switch and addresses the viewer with curious tales. The view from the top of the hill is remarkable, and was commented upon by no less a traveller than Dr Johnson, who visited Hawkstone in 1774 and wrote:

> *By the extent of its prospects, the awfulness of its shades, the horrors of its precipices, the ideas which it forces upon the mind are the sublime, the dreadful, and the vast.*

Today Hawkstone Park offers a rigorous and fascinating walk around and about the hillsides and still presents extended views with horrendous precipices!

Whitby Abbey

Yorkshire, OS NZ 8911

THE JAGGED sandstone ruins of Whitby Abbey dominate the skyline above the small fishing village that is often remembered today as the setting for the arrival of Dracula in Bram Stoker's celebrated book. The abbey was founded in AD 657 by St Hilda on land given by the Northumbrian King Oswiu, as a thanksgiving for victory over the feared King Penda of Mercia. The Synod of Whitby was held here in AD 663, finally establishing a still-divided church of England as owing fealty to Rome. The Danes destroyed the abbey soon after, and though it was rebuilt by the Normans, this too was demolished, and the ruins which now stand out on the headland date from the thirteenth century. In 1914 the German fleet shelled the building and wreaked further damage to its already battered walls. Its most famous inhabitant was the great English Christian poet, Caedmon, who wrote his wonderful 'Hymn of Creation' after miraculously receiving the gift of vision and poetry while a monk here in the seventh century.

Durham Cathedral

Durham, OS NZ 3407

TOWERING OVER the market town of Durham from its rock of 21 m (70 ft), and surrounded on three sides by the River Wear, this Norman cathedral is filled with memorials of ancient times. Begun in 1093 by Bishop William of Calais, it became the shrine of the Saxon St Cuthbert, whose tomb may still be seen in the cathedral. An interesting story is told of a certain short sword or falchion, which is held as part of the cathedral treasure. It is said to have belonged to one Sir John Conyers, who held the manor of Stockburn during the fourteenth century. In order to claim his right to this, Sir John performed the feudal service of offering his sword to the Bishop of Durham. The reason for this was said to be that Sir John had slain a serpent or dragon that was terrorizing the neighbourhood, for which service he was given the manor to hold in perpetuity. His family continued to honour the custom as late as 1826, when the falchion was presented to the cathedral. The story was celebrated in a stained-glass window at Stockburn Church, but this vanished sometime during the Civil War.

FURTHER READING

THERE HAVE BEEN literally countless books written about the legendary landscapes of Britain since the eighteenth century antiquarians rediscovered the enchantment of these magical places. Here are few that I found helpful in the writing of this book, which may help you explore the sites for yourself.

AE (William Russell), *The Candle of Vision*, Quest Books, 1965

ANDERSON, William, *Holy Places of the British Isles*, Ebury Press, 1983

BAIGENT, Michael and LEIGH, Richard, *The Temple & the Lodge*, Jonathan Cape, 1989

BARNATT, John, *Stone Circles of the Peak*, Turnstone Books, 1978

BAYLEY, Harold, *Archaic England*, Chapman & Hall, 1919.

BORD, Janet and Colin, *The Secret Country*, Paul Elek, 1976

— *Ancient Mysteries of Britain*, Grafton, 1986

— *The Enchanted Land*, Thorsons, 1995

BROMWICH, Rachel, *The Welsh Triads*, University of Wales Press, 1978

BROWN, George Mackay, *Letters From Hamnavoe*, Gordon Wright, 1975

BROWN, Peter Lancaster, *Megaliths, Myths & Men*, Blandford, 1976

CASTLEDEN, Rodney, *The Wilmington Giant*, Turnstone Press, 1983

DAMES, Michael, *The Silbury Treasure*, Thames and Hudson, 1976

— *The Avebury Cycle*, Thames and Hudson, 1977

DAMES, Michael, *The Silbury Treasure* London, Thames and Hudson, 1976

DARVILL, Timothy, *Ancient Britain*, Automobile Association, 1988

DAVIES, Hunter, *A Walk along the Wall*, Quartet Books, 1976

ELLIS, Peter Berresford, *A Guide to Early Celtic Remains in Britain*, Constable, 1991

EMBLETON, Ronald and GRAHAM, Frank, *Hadrian's Wall in the Days of the Roman Empire*, Frank Graham, 1984

FORD, Patrick K., *The Mabinogion and Other Medieval Welsh Tales*, University of California Press, 1977.

GRINSELL, Leslie V., *Folklore of Prehistoric Sites in Britain*, David & Charles, 1976

HANNIGAN, Des, *Ancient Trackways*, Pavilion Books, 1994

HAWKES, Jacquetta, *A Land*, The Cresset Press, 1951

LINES, Marianna, *Sacred Stones, Sacred Places*, Saint Andrew Press, 1992

MACSWEEN, Ann and SHARP, Mick, *Prehistoric Scotland*, B.T. Batsford, 1989

MALONE, Caroline, *Avebury*, B.T. Batsford, 1989

MALORY, Sir Thomas, *Le Morte d'Arthur*, Penguin Books, 1978

MATTHEWS, John (with Chesca POTTER), *The Aquarian Guide to Legendary London*, Thorsons, 1993

Opposite:
Robin Hood's Stride, Derbyshire.

MATTHEWS, John, *King Arthur's Britain*, Cassell, 1995
— *Robin Hood: Green Lord of the Wildwood*, Gothic Image Books, 1995
— *The Druid Source-Book*, Cassell, 1996
MATTHEWS, John and Caitlin, *A Fairy Tale Reader*, Thorsons, 1993
MUIR, Richard, *Shell Guide to Reading the Celtic Landscape*, Michael Joseph, 1985
— *The Stones of Britain*, Michael Joseph, 1986
NEWMAN, Paul, *Gods and Graven Images: The Chalk Hill-Figures of Britain*, Robert Hale, 1987.
PHILLIPS, Graham and KEATMAN, Martin, *King Arthur: the True Story*, Century Random House, 1991
READER'S DIGEST, *Folklore, Myths & Legends of Britain*, Reader's Digest Association, 1973.
ROSS, Stewart, *Ancient Scotland*, Lochar Publishing, 1991

SHARP, Mick, *A Land of Gods and Giants*, Alan Sutton, 1989.
SINCLAIR, Andrew, *The Sword & the Grail*, Weidenfeld & Nicolson, 1992
STEWART, R.J., *Robert Kirk: Walker Between Worlds*, Element Books, 1990.
— *Earth Light*, Element Books, 1992
— *Power Within the Land*, Element Books, 1992
STEWART, R. J. and MATTHEWS, John, *Legendary Britain: An Illustrated Journey*, Blandford, 1989
TAYLOR, Christopher and MUIR, Richard, *Visions of the Past*, J.M. Dent, 1983
THOM, Alexander, *Megalithic Lunar Observatories*, Oxford University Press, 1971
—*Megalithic Sites in Britain*, Oxford University Press, 1967
VANSITTART, Peter, *Green Knights, Black Angels*, Macmillan, 1969
WESTWOOD, Jennifer, *Albion: A Guide to Legendary Britain*, Granada, 1985

GAZETTEER

CAMBRIDGESHIRE
Wandlebury Dyke

CORNWALL
Men-an-Tol
Men Gurta
The Merry Maidens
Penhale Sands
St Michael's Mount
Tintagel Castle
Trereen Dinas

CUMBRIA
Castlerigg
Hadrian's Wall
Pendragon Castle

DERBYSHIRE
Arbor Low Henge
The Nine Stones
Robin Hood's Stride

DORSET
The Cerne Abbas Giant
Knowlton Circles

DURHAM
Durham Cathedral

HAMPSHIRE
The Great Hall, Winchester

HEREFORDSHIRE
Kilpeck Church

HERTFORDSHIRE
The Devil's Dyke
Royston Cave

LONDON
The White Tower

NORTH-EAST SOMERSET
(formerly Avon)
Stanton Drew Stone Circle

NORTHUMBERLAND
Chesters Roman Bathhouse
Hadrian's Wall
Piercebridge

ORKNEY ISLANDS
Gurness Broch
Maes Howe
Maes Howe Runic Slab
The Ring of Brodgar
St Magnus Cathedral
The Stones of Stenness

OXFORDSHIRE
The Rollright Stones
The Whispering Knights
Wayland's Smithy

SCOTLAND
Aberfoyle Faery Hill
Clava Cairns
Carn Liath Broch
The Eildon Hills
Robert Kirk's Grave
Rosslyn Chapel

SHROPSHIRE
Hawkstone Grotto
Hawkstone Park
Hawkstone Park Monument
The Stiperstones
Wroxeter

SOMERSET
Robin Hood's Butts
Wells Cathedral

STAFFORDSHIRE
Thor's Cave

SUSSEX
Arundel Castle
The Long Man of Wilmington

WALES
Bedd Taliesin
Bryn Celli Dhu
Caerleon-upon-Usk
Craig-y-Ddinas

Dinas Emrys
Kenfig Pool
Lake Bala
Llyn Ddinas
Owein Glyndwr's Footprint
Pistyll-y-Rhaeadr
St Winifrid's Well, Holywell
Snowdon and the Lake of Glaslyn

WILTSHIRE
Avebury
Silbury Hill
The Uffington White Horse
West Kennet Long Barrow

YORKSHIRE
Helmsley Castle
Richmond Castle
Sheriff Hutton Castle
Skipton Castle
Wheeldale Roman Road
Whitby Abbey

'She not any common earth
Water or wood or air,
But Merlin's Isle of Gramaraye
Where you and I will fare.'

A. E. Houseman

INDEX OF SITES

Companion volumes:

King Arthur's Britain
A Photographic Odyssey
John Matthews and Michael J. Stead

Holy Places of Celtic Britain
A Photographic Portrait of Sacred Albion
Mick Sharp